How to Play Better
DOMINOES

9/17/04

To Lawrence:

I hope it won't take "fish gall" to "open your eyes" to this wonderful game.

Enjoy!

How to Play Better DOMINOES

MIGUEL LUGO

Sterling Publishing Co., Inc.
New York

Dedication

This book is dedicated to those who were my partners and opponents, the "other three" who completed the foursome:

In high school: Speedy, Victor, and Frankie.
In college: Andito, Piti, and Don Cucho.
At present: Eduardo, Tito, and Jorge.
And in the future, my children: Rick, Javi, and Monica.

May we always continue to play and enjoy the great game of dominoes.

Edited by Peter Gordon

10 9 8 7 6 5 4 3 2

Published 2002 by Sterling Publishing Company, Inc.
387 Park Avenue South, New York, N.Y. 10016
Previously published by Sterling Publishing Co., Inc.
under the title *Competitive Dominoes*

Distributed in Canada by Sterling Publishing
c/o Canadian Manda Group, One Atlantic Avenue, Suite 105
Toronto, Ontario, Canada M6K 3E7
Distributed in Great Britain and Europe by Chris Lloyd at Orca Book Services, Stanley House, Fleets Lane, Poole BH15 3AJ, England.
Distributed in Australia by Capricorn Link (Australia) Pty. Ltd.
P.O. Box 704, Windsor, NSW 2756 Australia
Manufactured in the United States of America

Sterling ISBN 0-8069-8299-3

Contents

Introduction—Why Play Competitive Dominoes?

Competitive dominoes exercises your logical and reasoning abilities while at the same time allowing you to enjoy the camaraderie of friends. It is a game whose outcome depends mostly upon carefully following the plays made and trying to figure out the tiles of the other players. This mental challenge can be as satisfying as the feeling you derive from successfully solving a puzzle.

Dominoes has more portability than card games, since the tiles can't be blown away by the wind or damaged by water. Unlike board games, no special equipment (other than the tiles themselves) is required. It can therefore be played anywhere at any time.

When I was a child it seemed that only adults understood it well, so of course I wanted to grow up and learn to play it too! The sounds the tiles made as they were shuffled were strange music to my ears, as pleasing and delicate as wind chimes.

As teenagers, my friends and I would often gather in the school cafeteria during recess and play a few games. It was *the* game to play at the beach—I carried a plywood board to the sand at the water's edge and had to wait only a few minutes before schoolmates would come over and ask to play.

On special occasions we played "aquatic dominoes." We would travel to a neighboring coastal town, where a small barrier reef created a protected tide pool of calm water of not more than two feet deep. We would sit down and, with the saltwater up to our chest, play on my floating plywood board until the sun would toast us.

In college it was a popular way to break from studying. Every fraternity party had at least one table going on. Friday nights I went to the home of a friend who hosted a domino club for over 15 years. We ranged in age from 18 (myself) to 80 years old.

To this day, when I try to visualize a peaceful tropical night in the Caribbean islands, I close my eyes and hear these sounds: the steady trade winds blowing on the palm trees, the gentle surf against the reefs, the surprisingly loud and high-pitched cry of a tiny frog called a *coquí* ... and the distant laughter and soft tinkling of the shuffled tiles from a neighbor's dominoes game, carried by the quiet of the evening.

General Principles

The game of competitive dominoes is played with 28 tiles, evenly divided between four players who face each other across a square table. Facing players are a team.

The tiles are rectangular. There is an elongated groove that divides them into two equal halves, and each half is either blank or has a different number of pips, representing numbers. Most domino sets sold in toy or game stores are made of wood, painted black with white pips. The fancier game sets are made of hard plastic and are thicker. They also have a metal dot in the center that raises them from the playing surface, making it easier to shuffle or scramble them.

The tiles can be held in one's hand or stood on the table. A small rack made out of plastic or wood, called an *atril*, can also be used to hold the tiles. A special table to play dominoes can be bought with *atriles* already built into it.

The standard 28-tile domino set has seven numbers. They are the 6s, 5s, 4s, 3s, 2s, 1s, and those left blank. In dominoes, the blank is a number. There are seven tiles of each number.

A group of tiles that share one number is called a suit. For example, these tiles comprise the suit of 2s:

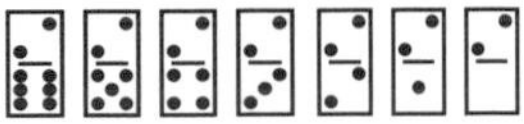

Notice that one of these tiles, the 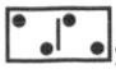, has a 2 in each side; this is called a "double" tile.

Each tile has a certain numerical point value. The 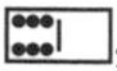, for example, is worth six points, while the  is worth 5 + 3 = 8 points. The more points a tile has, the "heavier" it is. Players sometimes refer to themselves as being "light" if their tiles carry few points, or "heavy" if they have many.

The sum total value in points of all 28 domino tiles is 168. Memorize this number, since it will become very important later on as you begin to play.

A match is composed of several games, each one of which wins points for a team. The match starts by shuffling the tiles while they're face down (the numbers not showing). Each player chooses and uncovers one tile, and the player with the highest point value (adding both sides) gets to lead off the first game. In case of a tie, the domino with the highest single number decides the lead player; for example, a 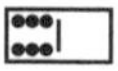 beats a . The leadoff position rotates counterclockwise on subsequent games.

The dominoes are shuffled again and each player now takes seven of them. The tiles in your hand should not be seen by the others, since this might be an unfair advantage for a team. If a player has drawn five or more doubles in his hand he is given the option of showing them and asking for a reshuffle of the tiles. This is allowed because such a combination is considered to be an almost-certain loss. Otherwise, a few moments are spent in organizing the tiles and studying them before play starts.

The designated lead player leads off with a tile and play proceeds counterclockwise. The next player must play a tile that matches either open end of the developing structure (known as the skeleton). Double tiles are played straddled across the line, the other tiles lengthwise. If the player whose turn it is to play has no tiles that match either open end, then he must announce out loud that he passes and play continues with the following player. A player who has a legal play cannot pass.

These are examples of legal plays:

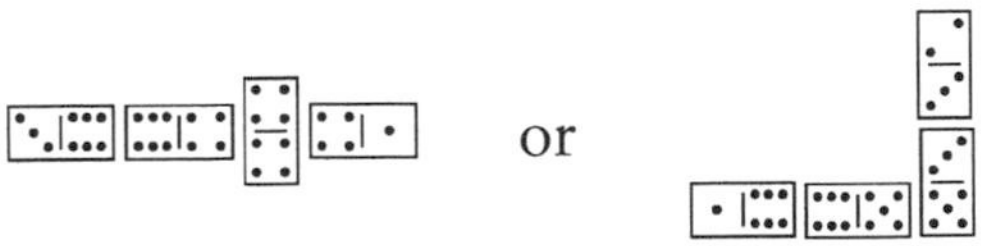

These are examples of illegal plays:

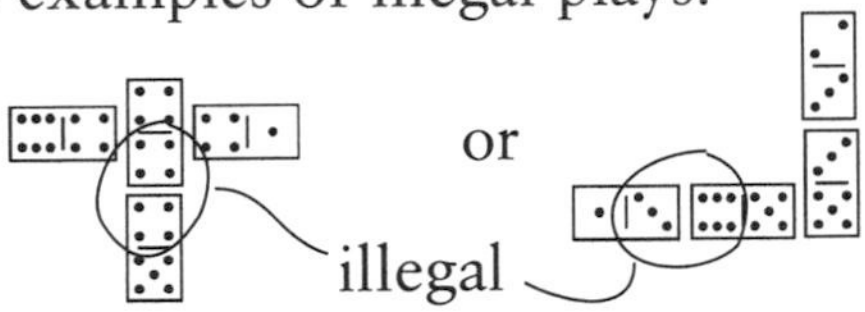

The game ends with one of two possibilities. If a player plays his last tile and is left with none, he is deemed the winner (having "dominated"). The unplayed tiles from the other three players are put together and their points are added. The total number of points is awarded to the winning team.

The other way to end a game is if a play is made so that no further plays are possible. In this situation the game is "jammed." The unplayed tiles of each team are added and compared to the other team's total. The *team* that has the lowest number of points is awarded the sum of all the unplayed tiles. If the sum is a tie the game is declared void and it is played over after reshuffling the tiles; the same player that started it gets to lead it off again.

Once a game ends and the points are counted, the tiles are again turned over so they're covered and a player from the losing team shuffles them. The player to the right of the previous lead player now gets to lead off in the new game. In this way every player takes turns leading off.

The score is kept by using two columns, one for the

points won in a game, the second one for the running total. The two teams are called simply "Us" and "Them." The player keeping the score writes down his team's points in the "Us" section. The left column represent the points won in the particular game, the right one is the running total. A match is played until a team wins 200 or more points. This is an example of what a score sheet might look like halfway through a match:

Us		Them	
12	12	31	31
26	38	15	46
55	93		

The Mechanics of Playing Dominoes

This chapter presents three sample games in order to illustrate the mechanics of playing competitive dominoes. You will find it most useful to follow along with your own domino set. Keep in mind that the players' choices may not be the strategically best ones to win the game. They are shown simply as examples of different types of plays and game endings.

Throughout this book we will identify the players in one of two ways. One way we'll call them is according to their sitting position around the domino table, using the cardinal points of a compass. North and South will therefore be a team competing against East and West. North is at the top, West on the left, South on the bottom, and East on the right.

The other label we will use relates to the *relative* advantage of a player over the others. The "lead player" is the one that has the fewest number of unplayed dominoes in his hand. He will, unless forced to pass, win the game by playing his last tile before any other player ("dominating" the game). The player with the next fewest number of tiles is the "2nd-lead." The next is the "3rd-lead," followed lastly by the "runt."

The seat labels are fixed during a match. The player sitting in the North position, for example, must keep that seat until the match ends by the winning team reaching 200 points. The relative leading labels, however, are constantly changing and it is critical to keep track of who's ahead at all times.

GAME 1: Example of a game that ends by one player dominating.

After shuffling the dominoes, each player chooses a tile and turns it over. South uncovers the  for 9 points, which turns out to be the highest tile of the four, so he leads the first game. These are the tiles as they are distributed after reshuffling:

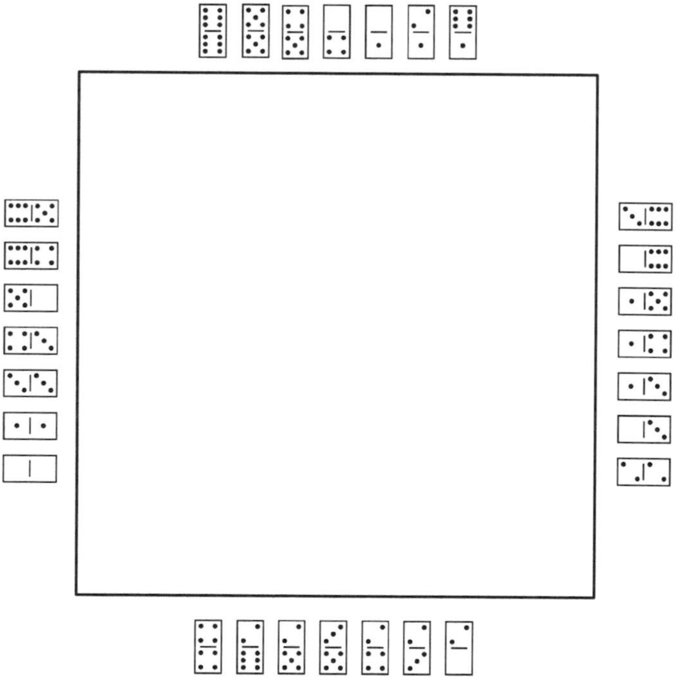

In this match North will be keeping score. He'll write down his team's points on the score sheet under the "Us" section. Remember that the unplayed dominoes are kept covered so the players can't see each other's tiles.

South leads with the  (we will study later how to choose the leadoff tile, for now just accept this play as a good one). East has only one 4 to play, the 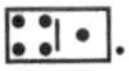. North can play on either the 4 or the 1. He chooses to play the 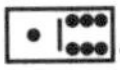. (Dominoes get added at 90° angles to others when there is no room left on the table to continue in the same direction.) West also has choices but decides to play the . This is how the board looks after one round of play:

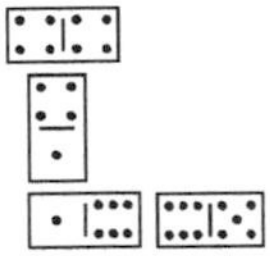

Since no one has passed, the leading positions haven't changed: South is lead player, East is 2nd-lead, North is 3rd-lead, West is runt. South now plays the . East has only one play, the 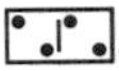. North chooses the  and West the . The developing structure now looks like this after the second round:

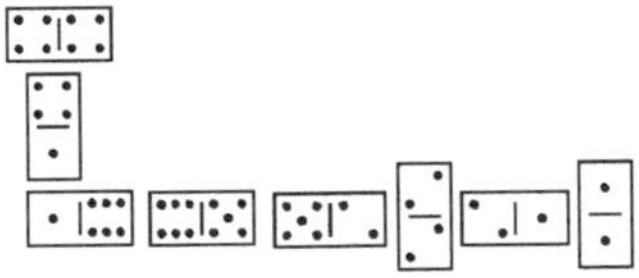

South has no 1s, so he is forced to play the 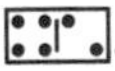. (You can't pass unless you have no play.) East has no 2s, so he plays the . North has no 2s or 3s, so he passes. West plays the 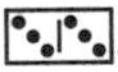.

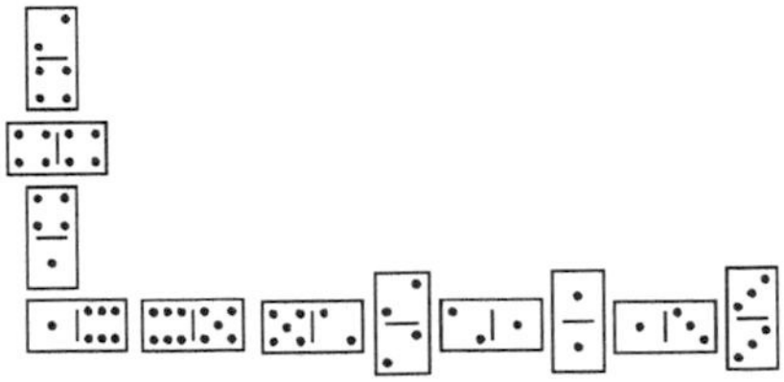

North, having passed, is now the runt, with the most unplayed tiles in his hand (five dominoes). His partner, South, retains the lead player position.

South plays the  on the 3; now both ends of the skeleton have a 2. This play is called "squaring" and is a strong attacking move, since it is more likely a player will pass if he's given only one choice to play—in this case a 2. (When both ends of the skeleton have the same number, it makes no difference from a strategical standpoint which end the next domino is played on.)

South has the only 2s left (five played + two in his hand = seven, a complete suit) so all other players pass. He gets to play again, this time the 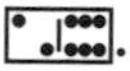. He is now both the lead player and the 2nd-lead. With only two dominoes left, he'll retain the relative advantage even if he passes once.

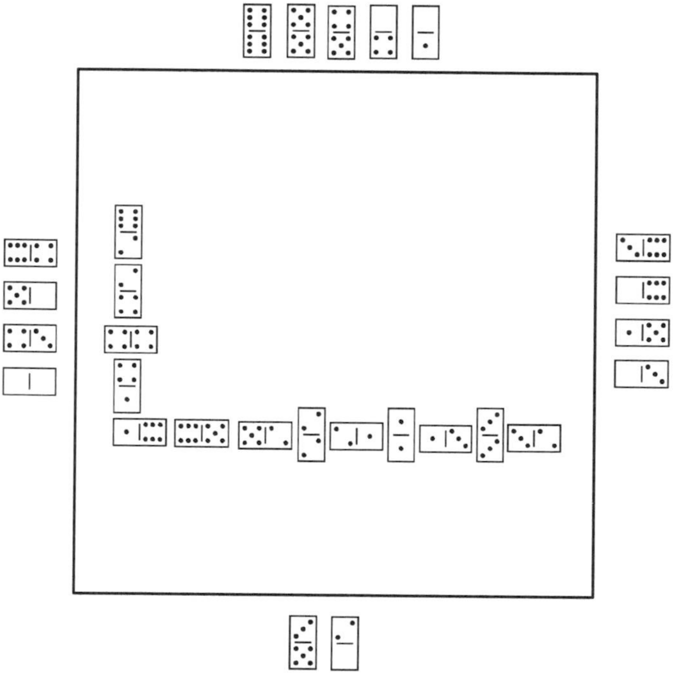

East follows with the 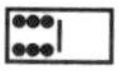 and North plays the 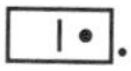. Now West passes and South, who is lacking 1s, must play the 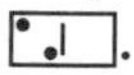. This particular tile, the last of its suit, is known as the "door" to that suit. He is said to be forced to throw the door to the 2s away.

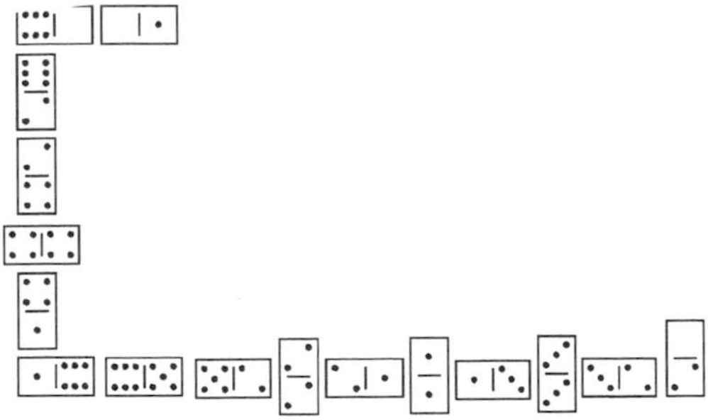

East plays the . North passes and West then plays the . South passes (no 4s or 1s) but still retains the lead player position. East plays the . North plays the  on the 5, squaring to 4. West now plays his only 4, the . South passes again, losing the lead player position, and East wins by dominating with his last tile, the .

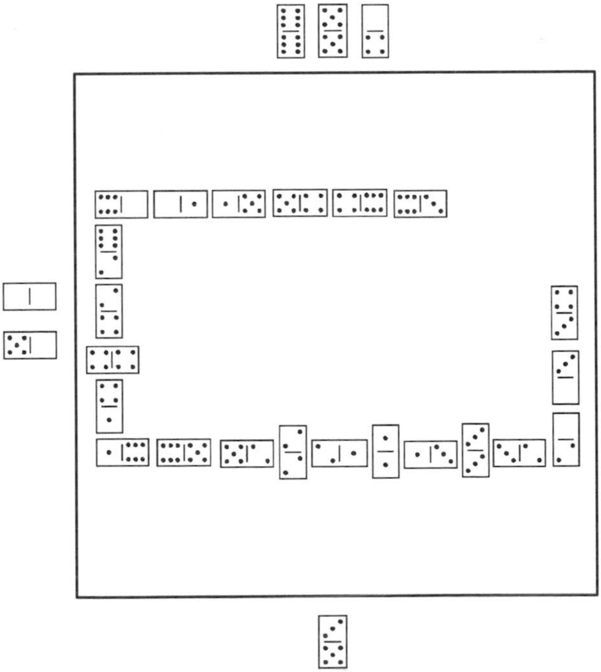

We now add the points from all the *unplayed* tiles and give the total to the winning team, East and West. This equals 39 points and the team is well on its way to its goal of 200 points.

GAME 2: Example of a game that ends with a jam.

All dominoes are turned over and shuffled by the losing team. The leadoff now belongs to the next player counterclockwise, East in our sample match. After picking up seven tiles, West observes he has 5 doubles, so he chooses to reject them and asks for a reshuffle. These are the tiles in the players' new hands:

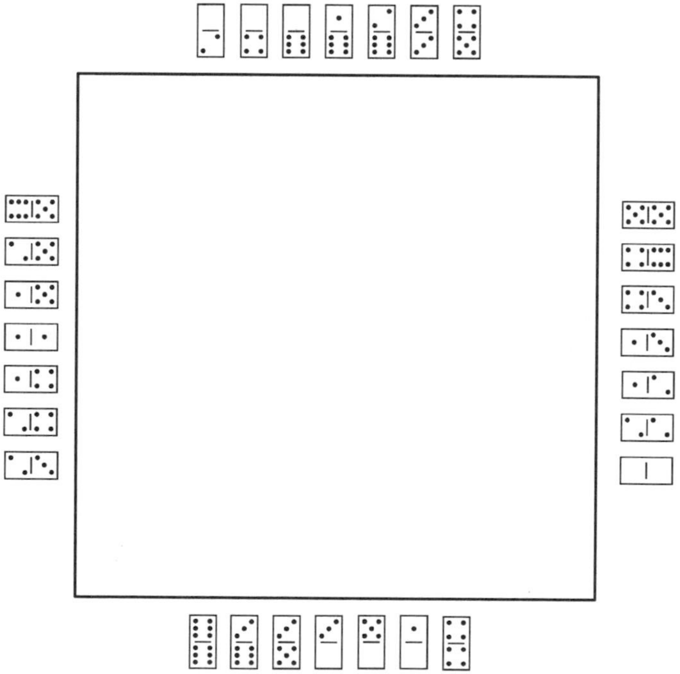

East leads off with the 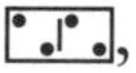, followed by the 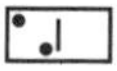 of North. West, having no blanks, plays the 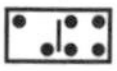 and South (who begins this game as the runt) decides to double with the . East begins the next round by playing the  and North attacks by squaring to blank with the 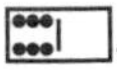. West has no blanks, so he has to pass. South plays the 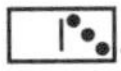. This is the way the board looks after two rounds of play (East retains the lead player position but his partner West has gone from 3rd-lead to runt):

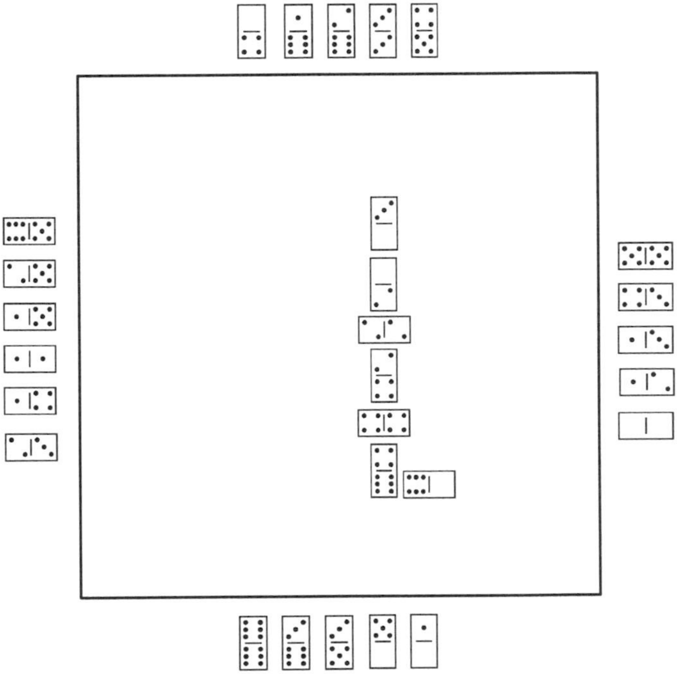

East decides to play the , followed by the 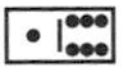 of North and the  of West. This play now allows South to square again to blanks, with the .

East still retains the lead player position. He now doubles with the 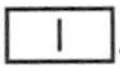. North plays his last blank, the 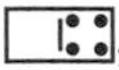, followed by the  of West. At this point we observe that South has the "jamming tile" (JT), the 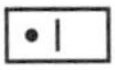. This is the seventh and last tile of a suit (the "door"), which can be used to jam the game so that no further play is possible. He plays it and squares to blanks, jamming the game.

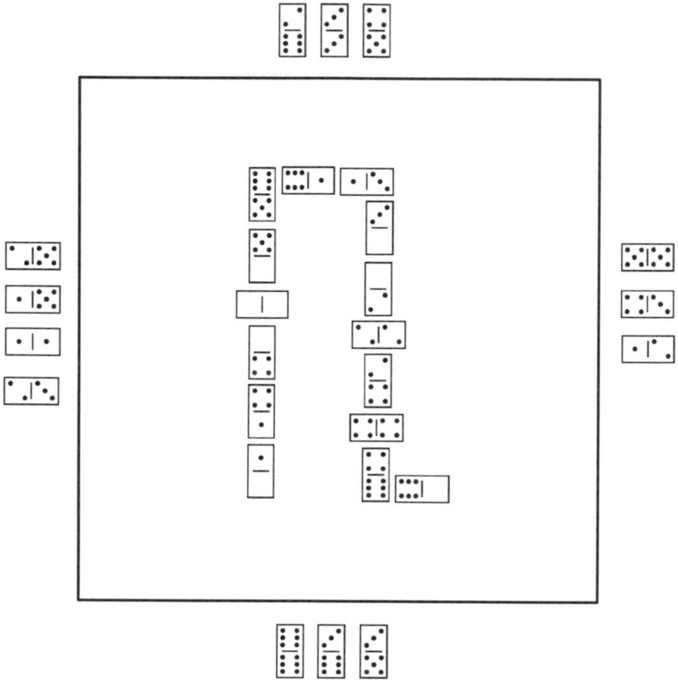

The game is "jammed." Now the points of each team's unplayed tiles are added together. The North-South team has a total of 52 points, and the East-West team has 40 points. This makes East-West the winner of 92 points. South's jam turned out to be a costly mistake!

GAME 3: Example of a game where doubles are eliminated from play ("hung").

One last example (on the top of next page) will set the stage for further discussion. Now North will lead off.

North leads with the . West follows with the . South squares to 6 with the . East plays his . The board after the first round looks like this:

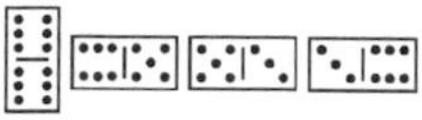

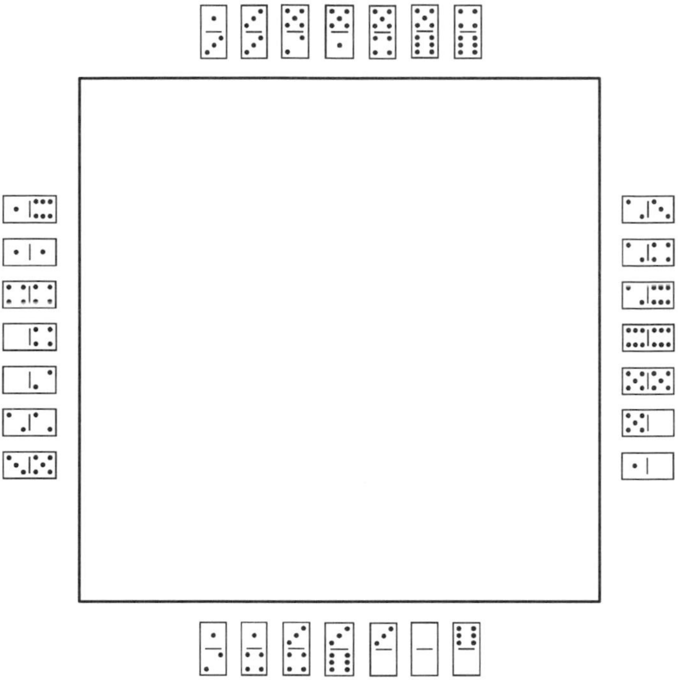

North must now cover the 6, one of his starting suits, and plays the . West doubles with the 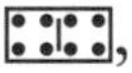, followed by the  of South and the  of East. The lead player position is still retained by North.

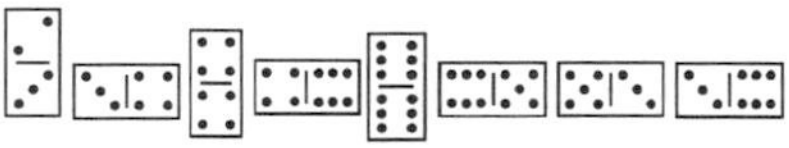

North now repeats his leadoff to the 5 by playing the . West, having no 5s, must throw away his last 6, the 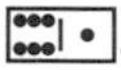. Now South repeats the 4 (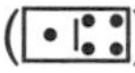), and East covers it with the 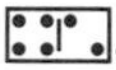.

The fourth round starts with North playing the 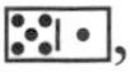, covering his 5 since he has no 2s. West doubles (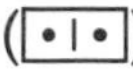). South plays the  on the 2, squaring to the 1s. East's only play is the 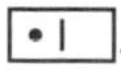. The skeleton now looks like this:

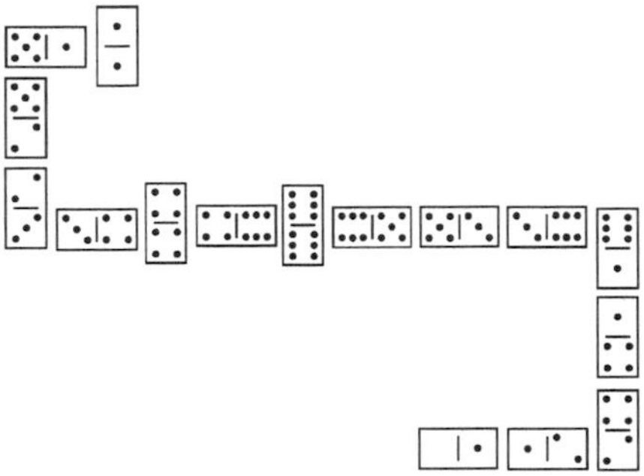

North still retains the lead player position. He now plays the , forced to do so because he has no blanks. West follows with the 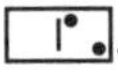. South plays the 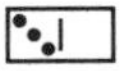 on the 3 and now we realize something: there's no way the  can be played! The other 3s are all played, so the double is "hung." North has it, so even if he's the lead player he can't win by dominating. Unless his partner can play all his tiles or a jam develops, this team will lose the game.

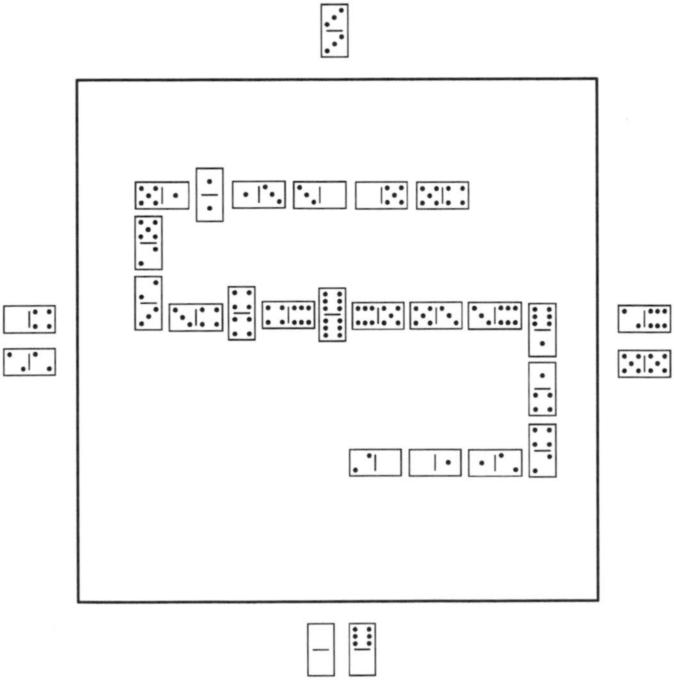

The round is completed by East playing the . North plays the , and now the is also hung! Another player is out of the game: this time East, who has the . (See the diagram on the previous page.)

West can now choose between playing either the or the . He should be able to tell his double is about to be hung, since there are five 2s already played. Also, the in his hand is the seventh 4 (the door), so no other player can play this suit. If the lead player passes he can win with it! He quickly doubles. South passes (having no 2s or 4s); East plays his . North (with the hung) passes, and West wins by playing the .

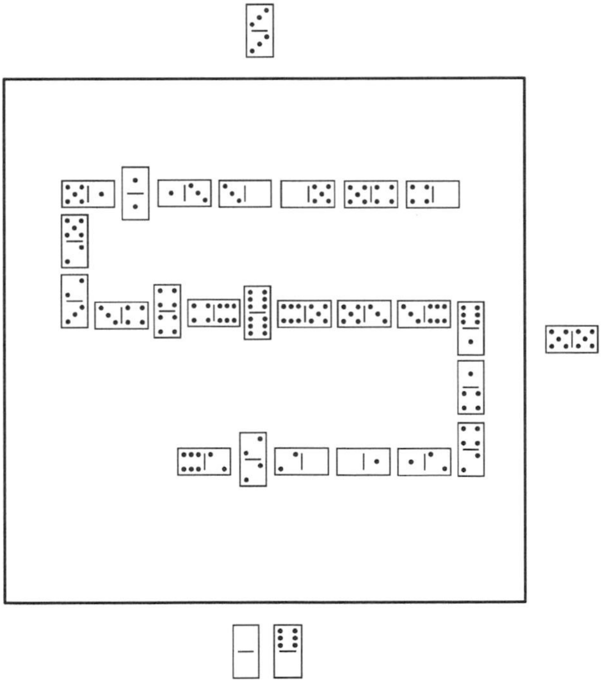

Remember that these games were played for illustrative purposes only. The plays made were not always the best ones, and there were many possible endings to each game.

The Laws of Dominotics

If you are a novice player you may need to read no further. I am sure that you can enjoy countless hours of fun playing this game with the basic skills covered already. Dominoes then becomes mostly a game of "a little luck and a lotta fun."

Somehow I know this will not satisfy you. You bought this book because you want to become a better-than-average player, or better yet, a champion domino player. If this is so, then read on.

After a few games are played (or observed), the smart player realizes that he can improve his odds of winning by a few simple strategies. Paraphrasing Isaac Asimov's Laws of Robotics, I present the "Three Laws of Dominotics." These laws help you win the game by guiding you in two ways: making your opponents pass, and making sure *you* don't pass.

First Law: A domino player must develop his own strong suits and help his partner develop his.

Second Law: A domino player must prevent the development of the opponents' strong suits, as long as this does not conflict with the first law.

Third Law: A domino player should play his tiles so as not to yield a suit, as long as this does not interfere with the first and second laws.

The First Law states you must develop your strong

suit, this being the one you have the most of. For example, if your hand looks like this:

the 4s are your strong suit.

You develop the strong suit by playing it and by not covering it unless forced to do so. If you have many tiles of one particular suit, then your opponents must have few of them and may be forced to pass (if they have none).

The Second Law states you must prevent the development of your opponents' strong suits. This is achieved by covering their suits with your tiles, and by *not* playing those numbers for them. If possible, you should also keep the opponents from playing their suits, usually by attacking them with your own.

This interference is always carried out unless it conflicts with the development of your own strengths (First Law).

The Third Law states you should keep from yielding a suit in your hand. To "yield a suit" means that after playing a tile you now have no other of that particular suit. For example, if you hold only the 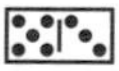   and need to play on a 4, then play the ; you still keep in your hand another 4 and another 3. If you play the , then you yield the 1s and next time that you're threatened by a 1 you'll have to pass.

Playing to prevent yielding a suit should be subordinated to the first two laws. In other words, it is not as important as developing your strong suit or preventing the opponents from developing theirs.

Mental Exercises

There are two fundamental abilities the domino player needs in order to excel. First and foremost is excellent memory, which is used to gather information about the game as it is being played. The second is the ability to take that information and, using deduction, figure out what is the best play to make from the tiles in one's hand.

An experienced player can usually tell, at any point in the game, who played a particular tile and in what order it was played. To help you do the same, I've written down the following mental exercises to develop your ability to recall.

These exercises are arranged in order of increasing difficulty. It will take some time to get good at them, but if you practice hard enough, the results will be self-evident when you rack up more wins.

1) When it's your turn to play, reconstruct the skeleton on the table, both the order as well as which player laid each tile.

2) Have another player pick any tile on the board at random, then try to remember who played it.

3) At the end of a game, pick up your original seven tiles from the skeleton.

4) Alternatively, pick up your partner's seven tiles.

5) Finally, pick up both of your opponents' original seven tiles.

Another important skill is to be able to count the

number of points on the board at any time in the game. Remember that the total number of points in the 28 tiles equals 168, so you can also know how many points are *unplayed* by subtracting:

168 – played points = unplayed points

This is helpful for two reasons. If a jam is contemplated, then knowing how many points are in the players' hands can be of critical importance (see Chapter 16). You can also astound your fellow players with a variation of this skill. I remember playing with an 80-year-old man who could keep a running total of the played tiles so that after the game was over he could nonchalantly announce the points won before I could even count the tiles. Now that's impressive at any age!

Analyzing Your Hand

The seven tiles you pick at the beginning of a game are your weapons in the upcoming battle. You should therefore study them carefully prior to playing the first one. If you analyze their combined strengths and weaknesses you can determine the initial strategy to follow.

The tiles can be reorganized after you get them, arranged in such a way that the suits are next to each other. This can help you "see" what you have in your hand.

Consider the following tiles in the hand of the lead-off player in our first sample game (Chapter 3):

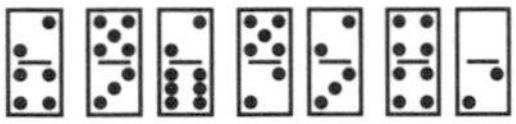

The strength of this hand is not readily apparent. If you reorganize them in this fashion,

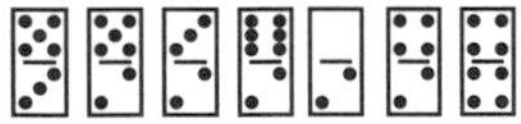

then it's easier to see that you have five 2s. There are only two others left in this suit, so there is a good chance you can make the other players pass by playing the 2s. You also observe you have no 1s. These can make you pass and must be avoided. Your initial strategy should therefore be to develop your 2s, while trying to prevent the development of the 1s.

Let's consider another hand:

After you reorganize them,

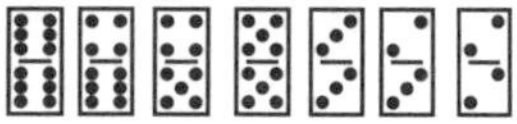

it's easier to see that this is a game with no particular strengths, but many weaknesses. There are no more than two of each suit represented, there are no 1s or blanks, and there are four doubles. As a general rule, the more doubles a hand has, the tougher it will be to win by dominating the game. This particular hand is also "heavy," or loaded with points.

Not every game can be won, and this hand really looks like a loser. The strategy here should consist of minimizing the possible damage, discarding as many of the points as possible. Since you can't mount an offensive campaign, you should support your partner's hand even at the expense of your own.

Here's another sample hand (after reorganizing):

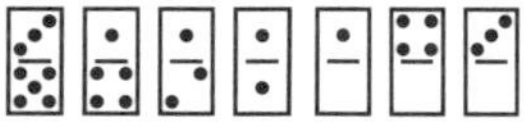

This hand is lacking in 6s, but is strongest in 1s and blanks. You should be thinking not only of developing the 1s and blanks, but also of the possibility of jamming the game. Having few total points means you are at an advantage if a jam arises.

A last example:

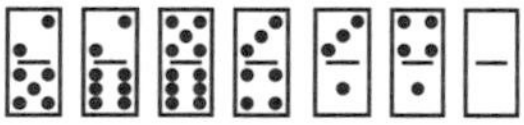

This hand has no particular strengths, having no more than two of any suit, but at least there are no suits missing. Although you can't mount an effective attack on your own, you can support your partner in his offensive and effectively thwart the development of your opponents' suits.

I should warn you that this technique of reorganizing the tiles in order to analyze your hand should be abandoned as more experience is gained. Some competitions forbid the shifting around of the tiles after picking them up. Worse yet, "shark" players can make very astute deductions about your tiles according to how you organize them and from where you play them. Notice, for example, how doubles often end up at the right or left end.

The Leadoff

The leadoff is a distinct advantage for the team that has it, since it allows them to develop their tiles first. For the lead player it can serve one of two purposes:

1. To start the attack with your strongest suit. This number will be the one your partner will try to support, while your opponents attempt to thwart its development. It is assumed (but not known for sure) that you have at least one other tile of this suit.

2. To discard from your hand a tile that is dangerous, either because it interferes with the development of your strong suit, or because it's a double you fear may end up getting hung. As a general rule, players usually lead with the heaviest double in their hand in order to discard points and to ensure they don't get stuck with that tile.

Both purposes may be achieved by the playing of the same tile. For example, if your hand is as follows:

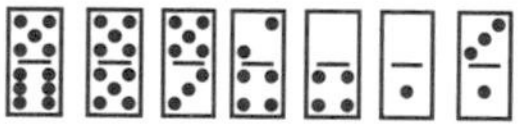

then leading with the  begins to develop the 5s as your strong suit and also gets rid of a potentially difficult double.

Keep these goals in mind as you determine the best leadoff tile in the following hands.

Example 1: No Doubles

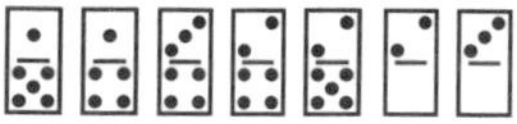

This hand has no double tiles. Its main defect is not having any 6s. Observing that there are three 4s and three 2s, you realize a lead with the 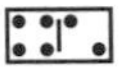 can develop the two strongest suits in your hand.

Leading with anything other than a double tile is called an "open lead." The other players will figure that the lead player either has no doubles to get rid of or has decided to keep the doubles for some particular reason. Subsequent plays will make clear which is correct.

Lead with the 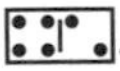.

Example 2: One Double

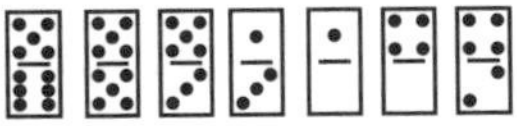

If you have two, three, or four tiles of a suit, including the double, then the logical leadoff is with the double itself. The only way a double in your hand can't be hung is if you have four or more additional tiles of the same suit. Even three others are not enough to be assured of its safety. You could play all three of them and they might all be covered by your next play. In this case, leading with the  not only assures it will not be hung, but also begins to develop your strongest suit.

The best lead is the .

Example 3: One Double

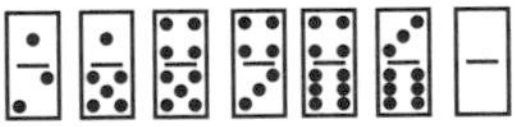

To lead with a double when you have no other tiles of that suit (for example, the 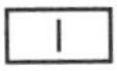 in the above hand) is called "leading a bluff." Although you are discarding a double, such a lead can sometimes be a poor move for several reasons. First, it sends the wrong message to your partner, and he might try to develop the blanks thinking it is your strong suit. Second, you lose the only blank you have (yielding the suit). Third, you may be leading with what may actually be the opponents' strong suit; in this case not only do you facilitate their play, but you lose what would have been an excellent tile to have in your hand. Finally, leading with the 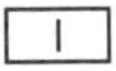 doesn't allow you to lighten up your point load, which could be important if a jam develops.

An open lead with one of the three 4s seems advisable. All things being equal, you should lead with the 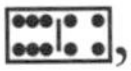, since there is another 6 in the hand and since it's the heaviest tile in the hand. Later in the game, if your partner sees you play the 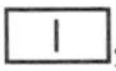, he should surmise that you have no other blanks (or you would have led with it) and must therefore protect you against them.

You should lead with the .

Example 4: One Double

Here your strong suit is the 5s, but the 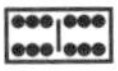 is a thorn in your side. A lead with it might not seem to be the most straightforward play. Leading with this double, however, would not be a bluff lead (since you have another 6), and it would eliminate the one bad tile in the hand. If you are forced to later cover the 6, you can do so with the  and attack with your 5s.

Leading with the 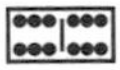 is a strong play.

Example 5: One Double

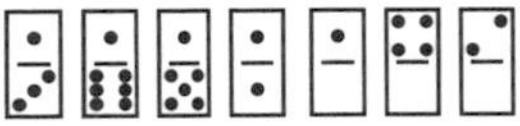

A dream of a hand! Five of a kind, with no other doubles and no suits missing. There are two possible ways to lead it.

The first is to lead with the . This way the other players must play a 1, maybe even both 1s that are missing, which would put you in great position with all the remaining 1s in your hand. There's even a good chance you will make the 2nd-lead pass immediately. It's a solid play and can't be faulted.

You could play otherwise, and lead with the . The  in your hand can't be hung, and you also develop your blanks. This will initially make the other players think you have no doubles, and hides the devastating power of the 1s to come. If you're later forced to cover your 1s, you have the double to use. Playing the  in the middle of the game will also tell your partner that you had *more* than four 1s to begin with, and none of the suit on the other side of the skeleton (or you would not have doubled then).

It's probably better to lead with the 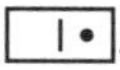.

Example 6: Two Doubles

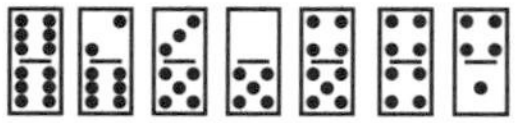

You have in your hand a 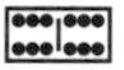 and a . It's not a memorable group of tiles. Since you have two other 4s, and only one other 6, a good option is to lead with the . Your hope is that, since you don't have the , perhaps another player will play it and allow you to double with the . Since you usually lead with the heaviest double in your hand, however, this might mistakenly tell your partner you don't have anything heavier than the  in your hand. Should you lead then with the ?

This is a hard choice to make and neither lead is wrong.

Example 7: Two Doubles

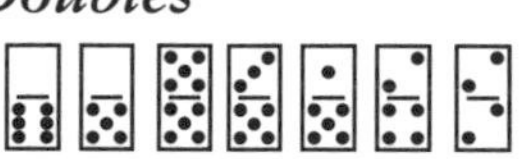

This is an easier choice. The 5s are clearly your stronger

suit, and a lead with the  develops them. It's unfortunate that you have the 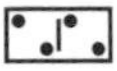 in your hand, but with a little luck you may still get to play it. You could lead with the 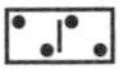 and hope someone covers it with the  (giving you a devastating advantage in 5s), but this is less likely.

The  is the best lead.

Example 8: Three or Four Doubles

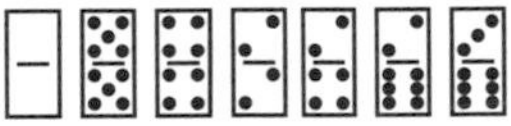

This is a terrible hand, where you hope your partner has good tiles and will "pull the hand" (take over the offensive of the team—see Chapter 13). The best lead might be a double, but not a bluff one. The  is by default the best choice, since it doesn't yield a suit.

Alternatively, there is a lead that has been popularized by William Almodovar. You lead with a non-double, *if* you still keep in your hand the doubles that match both ends. From the above example, this would be the  because you hold the  and the  in your hand.

This is tricky, since your partner must figure out your hand if there is to be a chance of winning. When you lead with an open tile, your partner examines his tiles. If he doesn't have either of the doubles, he can suspect an Almodovar's Opening; when the 2nd-lead doesn't double, your partner is almost assured you have those doubles. He can therefore play so you have opportunities to discard those doubles, or may decide his hand is best and pull the hand.

You should lead with the 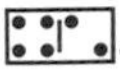.

Example 9: Five or More Doubles

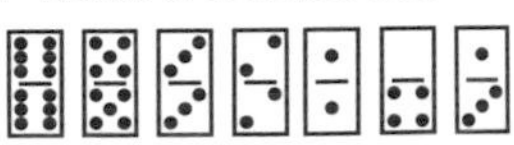

In my youth, it was often said that you could fold a

hand (rescramble the tiles) only if you had eight doubles. This of course meant you played with whatever hand you were dealt. Now that I'm older, and of a more delicate disposition, I'm happy that the rules allow folding a hand and rescrambling if you have five (or more) doubles. It's healthier for my blood pressure.

Nevertheless, you may be feeling adventurous or invincible and want to play this hand. If so, here's a tip I once garnered long ago: Lead with an open tile, if possible, in which you *don't* have either of those two doubles. It's the opposite from the Almodovar's Opening. The confusion you'll cause and the expression on the other players' faces as you play double after double may be the highlight of the match. Lead with the , sit back, and enjoy the ride!

Keeping Track of the Tiles

It is important to be able to keep track of the tiles as the skeleton is built. This applies both to the played and unplayed tiles, and both your team's as well as your opponents'.

Consider again the lead player's hand in the first sample game:

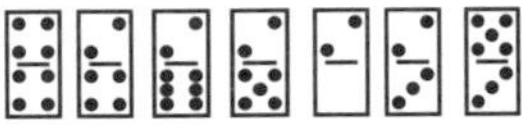

Not only is he aware of the five 2s he has, he should also realize the  and the  are the missing 2s. As the game is played, he keeps looking out for their appearance. He should also try to get them played as quickly as possible, so he'll have the last 2s left (First Law—develop your strong suit).

If you also keep track of the opponents' tiles, you may prevent their attacks (Second Law—obstruct the opponents' suits). Here's an example (see next page).

At this stage of the game you've figured out the player to your right (following you) is attacking with the 4s. You now must play a blank, and if your opponent plays a 4 and attacks, you will lose. Which one should you play?

Looking at the board you can see there are five 4s played and two missing, the  and the 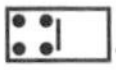. If you double with the 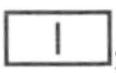, the 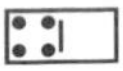 can be played and you'll lose. Playing the 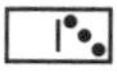 guarantees that no 4 can attack at that moment.

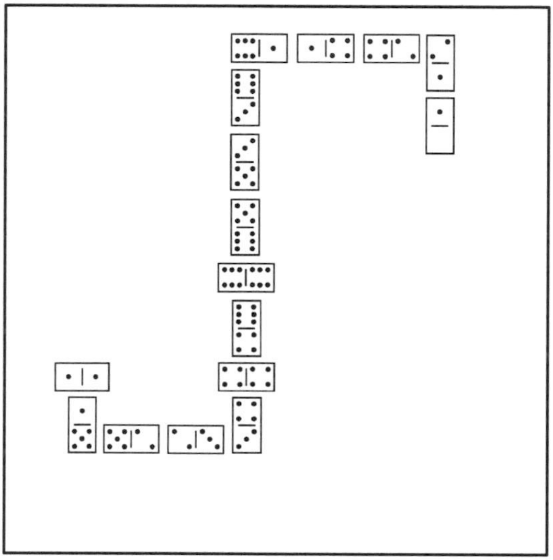

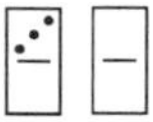

Blocking the opponents' plays can only be effectively carried out if you constantly keep track of those tiles not played. Here's another example.

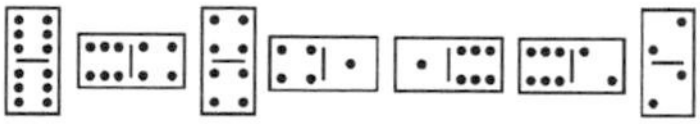

You are the runt and are holding

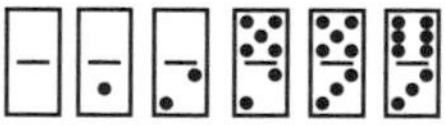

in your hand. The opponents led with the 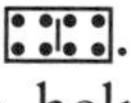. Your partner played the first 1, and you'd like to help him develop this suit. How can you help him to play the 1s?

Keeping track of the tiles you don't have, you realize there are four 1s unaccounted for: these are the , the 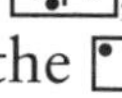, the 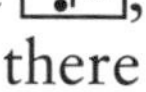, and the 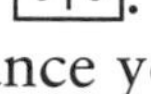. If you play either the 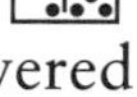 or the  , there is a chance your tile might be covered with a 4 (the  and the 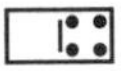 are missing) and your partner would be faced with a 6 on one side and with a 4 on the other. He wouldn't be able to play a 1 (the 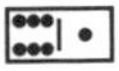 and the  are already played).

If you cover the 6 with the 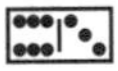 then both ends of the skeleton give him the opportunity to play a 1, either the  or the . The next player can't cover both ends in one play.

Now for a final example:

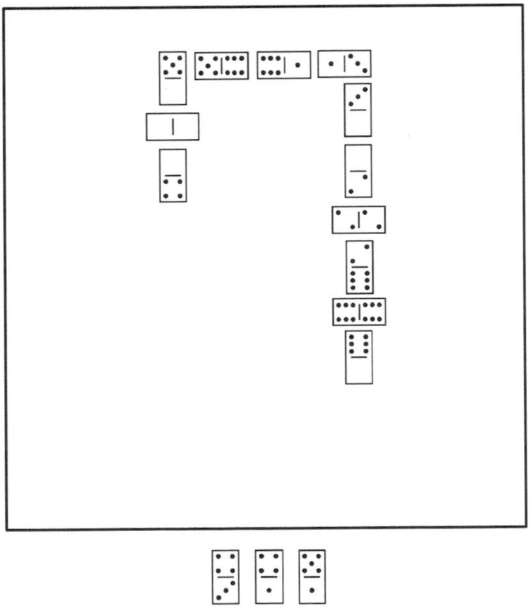

Let's say that your partner holds the door to the blanks (the last one), and you think your team can win a jam. Looking at the skeleton you should be able to tell the door is the 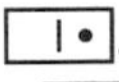. In that case, you can play the 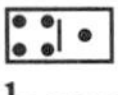 instead of the 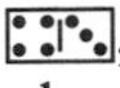, hoping the next player may not have a 1 (or might double on it) and your partner can then jam the game with the .

However, if the player after you holds the door and you think you'd lose the jam, play the to prevent it.

Cover, Repeat, and Square

The phrase "cover, repeat, and square" is often heard when beginners are first taught the strategy of the game. It is a very simplistic theory and yet it underlies most of the plays. If we were to compare dominoes with playing basketball, for example, then the equivalent strategy would be to say that to play it you need to "block, dribble, and shoot." Obviously basketball is more than those strategies, and yet how can you win unless you're able to do them well?

Cover: This means to play a domino tile on one side of the skeleton to cover that particular number. What is this number you are supposed to cover? The number to cover is the strong suit of your opponents.

Here's an example:

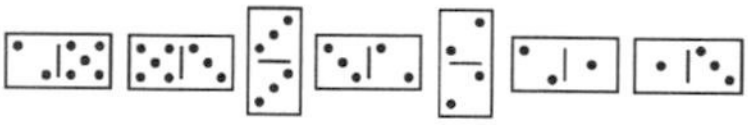

In this game you started as the runt, or last player. The lead player led with the  and the 3rd-lead has just played the . Since the opponents appear to be playing the 3s, and there's a 3 on one side of the skeleton, then it's logical you should "cover" this number with a tile of your own. If you don't do so, the lead player might be able to play a 3 and make your partner pass, or they might end up with a crucial door.

If your partner has no 3s, he'll be forced to play on the other side of the skeleton. In doing so, he may not be able to develop his hand, or perhaps he'll be forced to cover his own strong suit. He might have to play a tile that allows the next opponent to attack—and then it might be your turn to pass.

What if the only 3 you have is the  and it's also the only 4? You should not worry about yielding two suits (Third Law). Preventing the development of the opponents' suit (Second Law) is a higher priority.

What if you see the opponents developing a suit and you realize you might be able to play that same suit yourself? In the above example, what if you had in your hand both the  as well as the ? You might decide not to cover but to leave the 3 open, hoping to keep one or both of the doors.

This style of play is called "building a house." It means you abandon your partner to the tender mercies of the opponents, trying to get them to play for you without realizing it. The danger is that you can't expect much help from your partner, since he might now be unable to develop his game and still be trying to thwart the 3s from being played. We will discuss this style of playing in Chapter 14. For now, understand that the straightforward player would expect you to cover that 3 to follow the Second Law.

Covering prevents the development of the opponents' dangerous suits, and is therefore a *defensive* move (Second Law).

Repeat: This means to play a domino tile on one side of the skeleton to present a number for the second (or third) time. Here you're trying to play to your own or your partner's strong suit. (The numbers above the dominoes indicate the order in which they were played.)

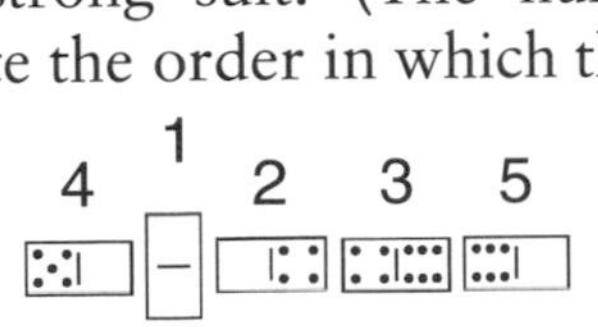

In this sample game, the lead player started with the 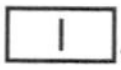. At the first opportunity he had, he "repeated," playing the 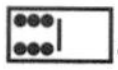. This signals to everybody that his strong suit is the blanks.

Not unexpectedly, the 2nd-lead doesn't have any more blanks and is forced to play on the 5. He has two of them, the  and the . He thinks a little before playing (to let his partner know he has at least one other 5), then plays the . He is repeating his 4s, since his first play was the 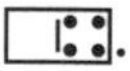.

The  would be a weak play, since it would allow the next player to repeat the blanks if he has the . On the other hand, repeating the 4s with the  ensures that the 3rd-lead won't be able to do so, since the 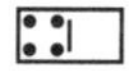 has already been played. Since it's the second time the 3rd-lead sees the 4, it might be too strong for him; he might not have any more 4s and be forced to cover his partner's blank.

What if the  is the last 4 that the 2nd-lead has? Should he repeat the suit even if it's not his strongest one? This is a tough situation, and you can play it one of two ways.

You can think for a long while before playing this tile. When your partner sees you repeating (and knows that this is usually a good move) he'll understand that if you had to think about it, there was something about the play you didn't like. You either wanted to play a double, but decided that repeating was a better move, or else you have no more 4s. If your partner understands your hesitation, he can study his own tiles and decide if he has the majority of the 4s or not. It is then his decision whether to proceed with their development or not.

Otherwise, after thinking about it for a while, play some other 5. Your partner will understand that either: a) you don't have the , or else b) you have it but the

4s might not be your strongest suit. Either way, the long "thought" tells him you had problems deciding the best play to make, and alerts him to potential trouble in your hand.

Repeating is the best way to develop a strong suit, and is an *offensive* move (First Law).

Square: This is the most powerful weapon you have to make an opponent pass. "Squaring" means you play a tile so both sides of the skeleton have the same suit. The tile you use to do so is known as the squaring tile, or ST. For example:

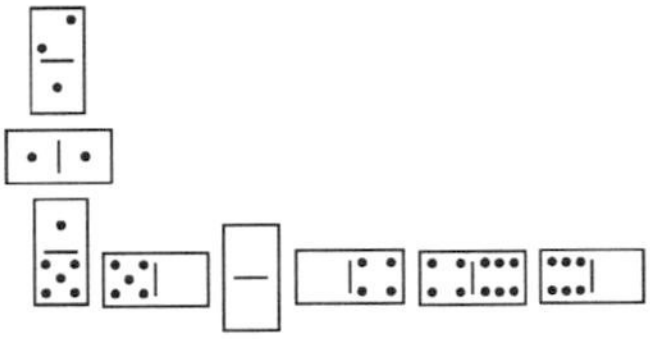

You're the leadoff player and you led with the 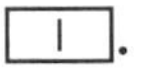. If you play the 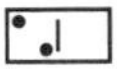 on the 2, now both sides of the skeleton have a blank. You have "squared to blank."

If you have another blank in your hand (like the , for example), then there is only one other unaccounted for. Chances are that you will make the next player pass, and you'll be sitting pretty with the door to the blanks.

Squaring is the most effective way of developing a suit. This is why the opponents should always try to prevent you from doing it. It is also the most effective way of thwarting your opponents. Consider if the above game had developed in the following way:

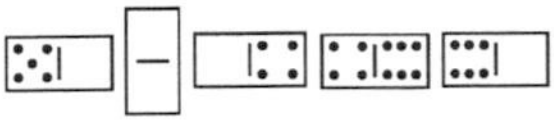

You led with the blanks, and repeated with the 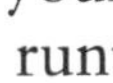. The 2nd-lead now repeats his 4 with the  , and your partner has to cover your blank with the . The runt now squares to 4 with the 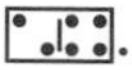.

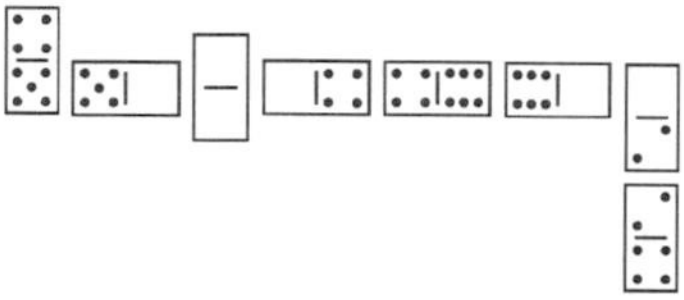

This square was extremely powerful. It prevents you from playing a blank and attacking. Your partner doesn't have any more 4s, or he wouldn't have covered your blank with the 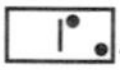. If you don't have any 4s, you now pass and lose the lead player position. Worse yet, the opponents will be able to play the 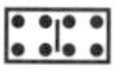 (most likely in the 2nd-lead's hand), and retain two doors!

Sometimes you're forced to square not to your strong suit but to the opponent's. Here's an example:

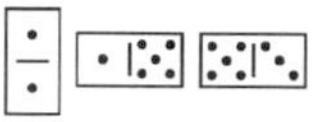

You're the runt. You have the  in your hand and must play it, since you have no more 1s or 3s. Do you square with the lead player (who led the ) to 1s, or with the 3rd-lead to 3s?

It may be satisfying to square to 1 and watch the lead player have to cover his own suit. Unless you suspect he led a bluff, that's about all the satisfaction you're going to get out of this play.

If you square to 3, you know your partner won't have to face another 1 this round. It's possible you might even make the lead player pass, making your partner the new lead player. The  will come out, though, and it's usually in the hand of the opponent who played the 3 first.

Either way, you see the square in this situation is a weak play. I usually square with the 3rd-lead (to 3 in this example), and hope to make the lead player pass.

Here's another situation. You're the lead player now, and must square with one opponent or another. (Again, the numbers above the dominoes indicate the order in which they were played.)

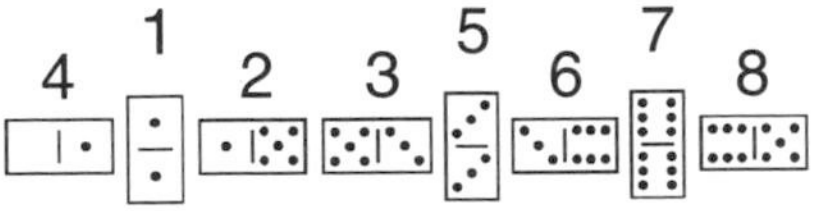

You hold the  and it's your only tile in either suit. Should you square to the 2nd-lead's 5s, or to the runt's blanks?

One answer is that, if you're the lead player, the one who can hurt you (make you pass) is the runt and you should therefore square *against* him by playing on the blank end.

You hope that by the time the play comes back to you, the 5s may be covered up again. Of course, the  will come out and your partner probably doesn't have it. Indeed, a common occurrence is that the 2nd-lead doubles with the , and your partner passes to 5s. Now the last player must cover the 5 and you'll have a different suit to play on.

Another way is to square to the runt by playing on the 5. It's likely your partner has a blank, since he hasn't played any yet. The 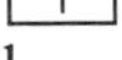 is probably in the runt's hand; the 2nd-lead will either pass or play a fresh tile to your partner. If the 2nd-lead does play a blank, for example the 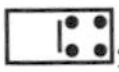, your partner should now cover the blank on the other side of the skeleton immediately. This opens the game for you to continue developing your suit.

Which opponent you square with depends on the strength of your hand. If you think you can win it, you'll square with the player following you, even if your partner gets in trouble. If your hand is not a strong one, you'll square with the player preceding you in order to open the game for your partner. And if you do the latter, and your partner knows your strategy of the game, he'll understand you're telling him, "My game isn't great. I'd rather you lead, if you can."

Squaring can therefore be seen as both an *offensive* as well as a *defensive* strategy.

How to Communicate with Your Partner

Very infrequently your hand can be so strong, so overpowering that you can win on the strength of your tiles alone. Most games, however, are won when your tiles and those of your partner can complement each other. In this fashion a team can make the opponents pass more often, while your team may develop two or even three suits.

By now you've gathered that a lot of decision-making involved in playing dominoes requires you to have at least an idea of the tiles that the other players have in their hands. This is not an easy matter. The opponents won't tell you, and sometimes will make plays to confuse you. Your partner is the only one with a vested interest in conveying to you the contents of his hand. How can you tell each other the tiles in your hands?

The one allowed way to convey information between partners is by the act of thinking—specifically, how long it takes you to play a tile is supposed to tell something about your hand. Of course, in order to understand each other, you and your partner must use the same "thinking conventions." Let's explore how you can use this tool.

You first begin to use it with your lead. If you only have one double, and it's going to be your lead tile, then play it quickly. This tells your partner, "My game is fairly good. I may have no other double."

A medium-length "thought" before leading a double says: "I have more than one double and my game is fair but may not be very strong."

A prolonged thought followed by a double tells the partner you either have a lot of doubles (3 or 4), and have a poor hand, or you might have led a bluff (not having any others of the suit whose double you just played) for reasons to be determined as the game progresses.

A prolonged thought followed by leading with an open tile (one with a different suit in each end) says you either have a poor game with many doubles—and decided to use Almodovar's Opening (see Chapter 7)—or you may truly have no doubles in your hand and yet were unsure which was the best lead. Perhaps you did have one double in your hand with no others of that suit, toyed with the idea of leading a bluff, but decided not to.

All this information can be (legally) expressed simply by varying the time used to think before playing the leadoff tile. Of course, the opponents will also pick up this information, and will try to use it against you. I still believe it is more important to let your partner know your hand, since he's the only one who has an interest in helping you.

Thinking time is used throughout the game, not just to lead off. For example, if the lead player leads with a  and you, as the 2nd-lead, have only one 5, then play it quickly. This tells your partner he needs to cover the 5 as soon as he can. Your tile was a forced play, so the suit you show may not be your strong one.

If you think on the , then it means you have two 5s—maybe even three if you think for at least ten seconds. Since you took the time to decide which 5 to play, the tile you played is probably your strongest suit and your partner should help in its development. He also shouldn't feel forced to cover the  that the lead player led with, since you have at least one other to defend yourself with.

Let's follow a game for two rounds, to see this concept in action. You're supposed to lead and, after thinking for about five to ten seconds, you play the . This tells your partner you have at least one other double. You probably didn't lead a bluff, or you would have thought for a little longer before leading.

The 2nd-lead, after a brief pause, plays the . If he's playing with the "thinking time" conventions, then you assume he probably has another 6. Remember, though, you can only truly trust your partner; the opponent could be bluffing. Your partner now plays the  rapidly; this must be his only 5. The last player also plays the 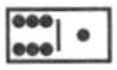 rapidly.

You quickly play the ; your partner now knows what your other double was. The next player plays the . The board now looks like this:

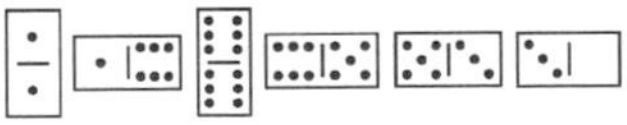

Now your partner thinks, and thinks some more. Then he plays the 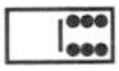. What does this mean?

He knew the 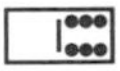 was a good move, since it would have repeated your leadoff suit, developing the 6s. And yet he was reluctant to play it. This must mean he had other blanks, and he must have really hated covering the 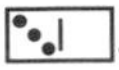. Perhaps he even has the 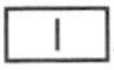. If so, he made a decision: he's sacrificing a strong suit, even putting his 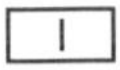 at risk of getting hung, to support your hand. You now start considering how to get him to play his blanks, especially if you happen to have some in your hand.

This is how partners can help each other and, in so doing, defeat their opponents.

What if you need to think because you have choices on both ends of the skeleton? For example, you hold the 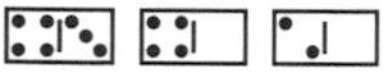 in your hand and the skeleton looks like this:

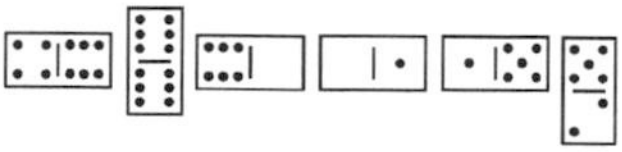

You need to consider whether to play a 4 or a 2. If you decide to play a 4, like the 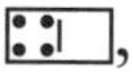, then a moderate pause to think before playing it conveys the message that you have other 4s. If you decide to play the 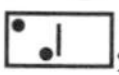, but realize the time you took to think this over will make your partner believe you have other 2s, then simply play the 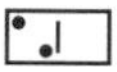 *quickly*. That is, take the tile in a quick movement and place it on the table with a definite, short action. The meaning of the quick action will be plainly understood: it's your only 2.

Sometimes it's okay to think even when you have no other choice but one play. It should be done to fool the opponents, when possible. Here's an example:

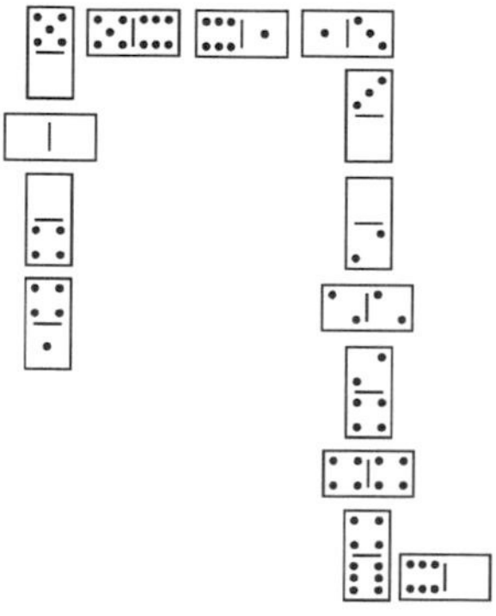

You suspect the player after you has the door to the

blanks, the 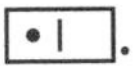. The only play you have is the , which will allow him to jam the game. You also estimate that the opponents will win this jam. You can bluff by thinking, then playing the —which may cause the opponent to fear you could be setting him up—and therefore decide *not* to jam!

Here's another example, where you can fool the opponents without confusing your partner.

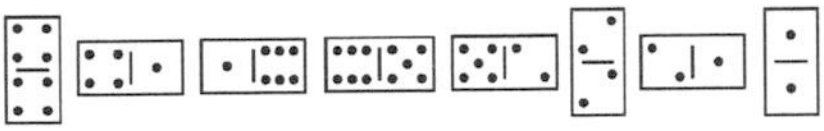

Let's say both opponents have passed on the 1, so they know you and your partner have the three 1s left. It's your turn and you are forced to cover your strong suit with your only 1, the 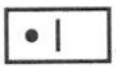. If you play it quickly then the opponents will know your partner has the last two 1s left, and can play to prevent him from playing them. By thinking for a while on your play, you can fool them into believing you have at least another 1, and your partner is amused by what he knows is only a trick.

This last setup can have another effect. If your partner plays one of the 1s he has left, the opponents will believe you must have the door and may unwittingly make it possible for him to jam the game!

You need to be careful of not only what tile you play, but also the speed with which you play it. You might have only one play possible, but if you stop to think about what has just been played, or what possible effect your play will have, then your partner believes you have choices to make. Still, you need to keep up with the development of the game. This is crucial.

How then can you achieve both goals; that is, use "thinking" to convey information while carefully analyzing the plays made? You do this by anticipating the tiles that may be played, much as the chess player figures out the next several moves he can make. Chapter 18 illustrates complete games and shows how to think ahead.

How to Play the Doubles

The doubles often play a crucial part in a game. By their nature, they are defensive tiles. They can't be used by themselves to attack an opponent or cover their suit, but rather to keep the present suit unchanged. They can also get hung, becoming unplayable.

Playing the doubles correctly sometimes leaves the realm of pure logic and begins to enter that of instinct. Here is where dominoes truly becomes a game of finesse and "gut feeling." Still, certain general principles about their play can be discussed.

A. When to Play the Double

Doubles are usually bad tiles to have in your hand. There are players who believe the team that has picked up four or more doubles should theoretically lose. Five or more doubles in one player's hand even allows him to ask for a new hand.

This means that, as a general rule, you should discard the doubles as soon as the opportunity arises. Consider the following example: you're the 3rd-lead. Your teammate led with the . The 2nd-lead plays the 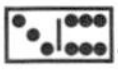. If you have the 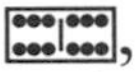, it should be played at this time. If you have this tile and don't play it, your partner will assume it's in one of the opponents' hands and will try to hang it.

Can you estimate the probability that a double in your hand will get hung? You can get a feel for it by looking at the rest of the tiles. Consider the following examples:

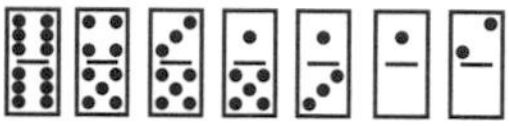

Here the 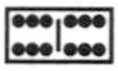 is the only 6 you have. There are six others out there in the other players' hands. It is unlikely the  will get hung, and it may even keep you from passing if you're attacked with the 6s.

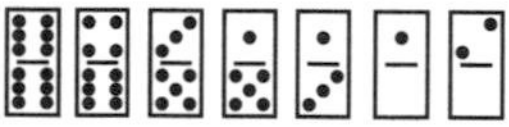

Having another 6 in the hand increases the chances of getting the 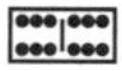 hung, especially since the  is your only 4, and you may be forced to play it on a 4 in the skeleton.

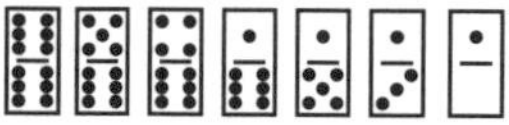

Two or three others with the double represent the highest danger. Three others is somewhat less than two, because if your partner can play just one 6, then you'll be assured of doubling. If the others are all in the opponents' hands, however, then any 6 you play can be covered and you might never get the chance to play the 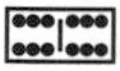.

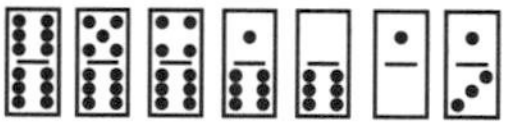

With four others, there is now no way your opponents can hang the double. Only you yourself can do it.

B. When Not to Play the Double

We've established that doubles are usually to be discarded at the first opportunity. Are there situations when you'd like to play them, but probably shouldn't? Yes, if a) there is a better play to make, or b) doubling would allow something bad to happen.

Here's an example. You, as the fourth player, are

given the chance to double on the 4. The lead player led with the and your partner played the .

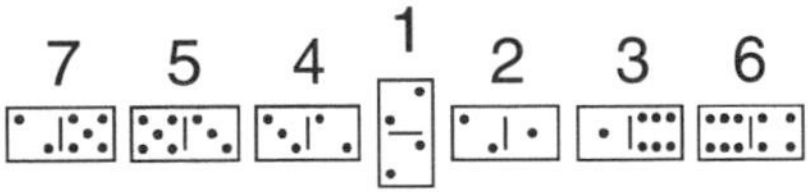

You have in your hand both the and the . Your first instinct would be to double, and yet you realize the 4 has been played for the first time and will probably not seriously threaten the lead player. Repeating your partner's 1 would represent an attack, so the is a better play.

Consider also that the is not played yet. Since the lead player started with the , you assume the 2s are his strong suit. If you double, he could the play the , squaring to 2 and attacking your partner.

Here's another example later in the same game, where doubling at the wrong time could lead to disaster. You have the choice of playing the or playing the .

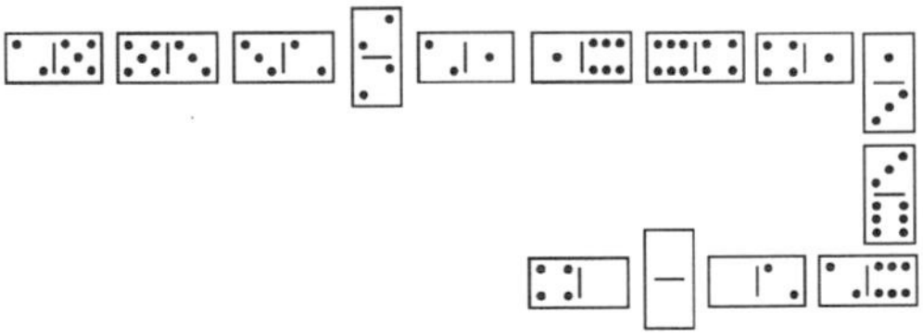

You're once again given the opportunity to double on the 4. This time the is not only missing—it's the jamming tile. You suspect your team would lose the jam so the is the best play possible.

The question may then be asked, is the only good double a dead double? Not necessarily—if it's the double of your team's strong suit. Having five of a suit, including the double, means you don't have to cover your own suit when attacked, since the double allows you to repeat it. It is thrilling when your partner squares to a strong suit, the opponent passes, then you double, repeating the attack and making the next opponent pass.

If you know a double won't be hung, doubling becomes optional. For example, let's say you're the fourth player and this is the skeleton:

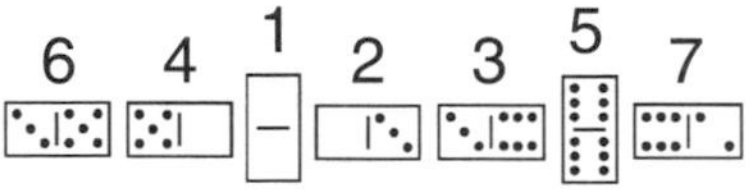

Your tiles are:

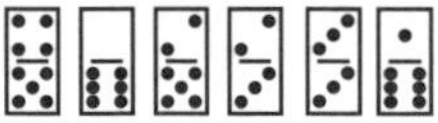

Doubling up on the 3 might seem like a good idea, but the  is actually a powerful weapon in your hand. Since your partner has played two 3s in a row (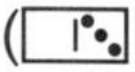 and ), it is probably his strong suit. The better play is to cover the 2 on the right with the , squaring with your partner to the 3s. This play may force the leadoff player to pass, making your partner the new lead player. You'll hopefully get to play the  in the next round.

C. *When to Pursue the Double*

If getting your doubles hung is a potential disaster, then hanging your opponents' seems like a wise strategy. There are players who are experts at this aspect of the game, and will doggedly pursue doubles to the death. Some will carry this persecution of the double to an extreme, hanging any and all doubles they don't have. This may prevent them from developing their game and may even get their partners in trouble.

How can you tell if you should hang a double or not? After all, if you're hanging a double, by definition you are throwing away the door to that suit that you might otherwise keep to yourself. As a general rule, if you're fairly certain your partner doesn't have that particular double, it's best to hang it.

Try to keep track of the doubles as the game is played. Here are two examples.

You are the 3rd-lead and your partner leads off with the . If you had the  in your hand you would play it, so your  tells your partner (if he doesn't have it) it's in one of the opponents' hands. This is one double that your team shouldn't hesitate to hang.

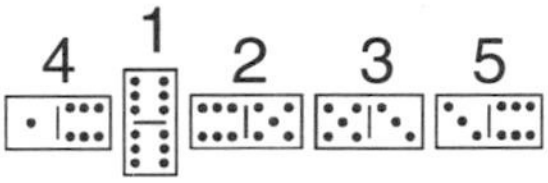

The runt plays the 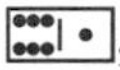, and your partner starts the second round with the . Since he didn't double with the 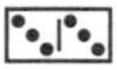 then it means he doesn't have it and you can hang it with impunity, right? Not necessarily—he may have the double, but decided it was more important to repeat the attack with the 6s than to double, and he hopes to be able to discard it later. Further plays will show which of the two possibilities was correct.

D. When to Hang Your Own Double

As strange as it sounds, you are sometimes required to hang your own double—the ultimate sacrifice! You should do this only if it's needed for your partner to win.

Let's say your partner has one tile left, and you know it's the . On the board there is a 5 at one end of the skeleton; on the other end is a 1, and you hold the last two 1s (the  and the ). By hanging your own 1 and playing the 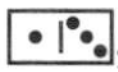, you assure your partner's victory, since the skeleton now has a 5 at one end and a 3 at the other—and your partner can't be stopped with the  in his hand.

Another example is when your partner is the lead player and he has the door to one end of the skeleton. You have the double and the door to the other side. If you double, you know your partner must discard his door, potentially costing him the game. You may then think that hanging your double might allow him to play on the other end of the skeleton, keeping his door for another round. This is not a sure thing, however. The player after you may still attack with his strong suit, and force your partner to discard the door anyway—making your sacrifice worthless.

You don't usually win by weakening yourself for the sake of your partner, but rather by you and your partner helping each other develop your strengths. You should therefore hang your own double only if you're somehow assured of a catastrophe if you don't. This is extremely difficult to predict beforehand, so you won't find yourself making the ultimate sacrifice often.

How Your Position Affects Your Game Plan

Should your game strategy be different if you're the lead player, 2nd-lead, 3rd-lead, or runt? On a very basic level you can think of the lead player and 2nd-lead as being the attacking players of each team, those who will first develop their strong suits. The 3rd-lead and runt are supportive players, who may need to sacrifice their own interests for the sake of their partners.

Although superficially correct, this generalization will not give you the consistent results that are needed in order to win. If this were true, the team would always win (or lose) according to the strength of the first two players, and this is definitely not the case. Let's therefore consider each position one at a time in more detail.

The Attacking Players
A. Lead Player
The lead player is the only one who has the luxury of choosing from all seven of his tiles and playing the one that helps him most. This advantage can't be taken lightly and choosing the correct tile to lead off must be done carefully (see Chapter 7).

If the tile he leads with is his strong suit (instead of playing to get rid of a bad double), then he must try to develop that suit. He must repeat it in order to keep the

2nd-lead off balance, hopefully until he passes. At that point his team becomes both lead player and 2nd-lead and his chances of winning increase significantly.

When feasible, he should try not to yield a suit (Third Law of Dominotics). He will therefore have a wider choice of plays and a better chance of preventing a pass.

Since few games can be won on the strength of one player only, he needs to look for opportunities to help develop his partner's tiles. If his hand is strong and he must choose between his partner's suit or his own, however, he'll prefer to develop his own game.

If his hand is weak, then he might discard the heaviest double as a leadoff, and somehow let his partner know he is in trouble (see Chapter 10). In this situation, it is he who should support his partner (the initial 3rd-lead) in the development of his hand.

B. 2nd-Lead

The 2nd-lead has to play off of the leading tile; his choices are more limited. He should still try to develop his strong suit as soon as possible, but he may not be able to do so until the following round, since he may be playing his first tile as a forced play.

If possible, the first tile he plays should be either his strong suit or a suit in which he holds a double (sometimes it's both at the same time). For example, if he holds the 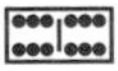 in his hand, and the lead was the , then a good play would be the 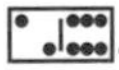.

He also should try not to yield a suit. He may need to do so, however, if it helps in the development of his team's strong suit.

Like the lead player, he should attempt to help his partner (the runt) by repeating his strong suit. Squaring to his partner's suit, especially if it's against his own, is the best way to say he'd like for the runt to take over the offensive. For example:

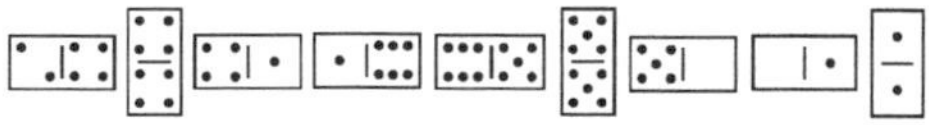

The leadoff was the . You, as the 2nd-lead, played the , and your partner, the runt, played the . At this stage of the game (third round) you hold the squaring tile, the 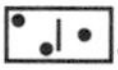. You know your game is weak and you'd like for the runt to take over the attack. You can do so by squaring to 2 (his first tile played) instead of to the 1s you first played. He'll understand immediately that you want him to take over.

The Defensive Players

A. 3rd-Lead

The 3rd-lead's main responsibility is to assist his lead-player partner. His first play is defensive, but he needs to begin showing his game and, if possible, his doubles.

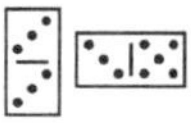

The leadoff was the , and the 2nd-lead played the . If the 3rd-lead has the , he needs to play it now; otherwise his partner will assume he doesn't have it and may try to hang it. If he doesn't have it, he should play his strong suit that has a double; for example the  if he has the 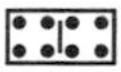 (and maybe other 4s).

In the next few plays he needs to continually scan for weakness in his partner, to know whether he should take over the offensive (a strategy called "pulling the hand"). If so, he starts to play as if he were the lead player, and the lead-player guidelines apply to him.

If no signs of weakness are apparent, then he's expected to fully support the lead player. One way he does this is by repeating his partner's strong suit. For example:

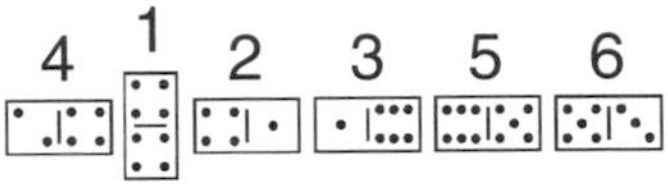

The 3rd-lead knows his partner, the lead player, played first the  and later the . The 4 could be the lead player's strong suit, since he led with it. He could have been, however, discarding a bad tile, so maybe the 5s are his suit (being the second tile he played). How should the 3rd-lead play now?

If he has the  then he should play it, since he's repeating the lead to 4s. If he doesn't have it but has the , he can repeat the second suit his partner played (the 5). If he has neither, but has the 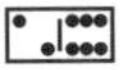 or the , then he should play one of them because he's now repeating his own first tile (the 6). If he has none of these, then he should play a double. If he plays *anything else* then the players should assume he has none of the above tiles. (Note: this is how you begin to guess the tiles in the hands of the other players—if they're playing logically! More about this in Chapter 15.)

The runt is in the best position to make the lead player pass or discard a door. The 3rd-lead therefore has to prevent the runt from playing his strong suit. To do this, always keep in mind the tiles that are not in your hand (Chapter 8).

Finally, if he can't attack or prevent the opponents from attacking, then he should look for ways to help the lead player play his own strong suit. For example:

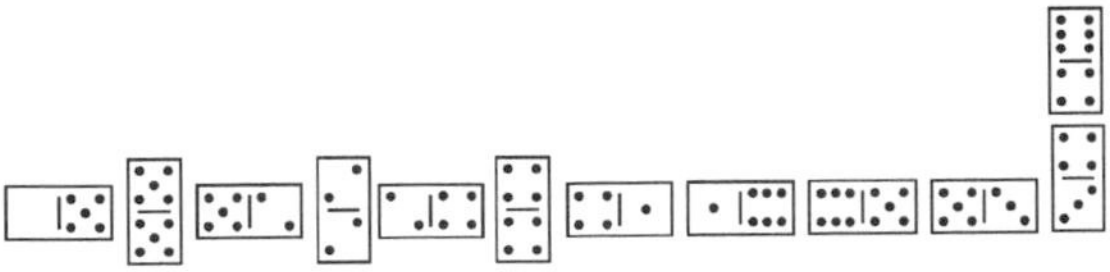

In the continuation of the above game, let's say that

the 3rd-lead has figured out that his partner did have a strong game to 4s, and he suspects that the lead player has in his hand the last two 4s. Looking at the skeleton he can figure out that they are the  and the . If he has the 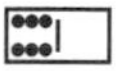 in his hand and squares to blanks on the 6, he's assured his partner of playing the 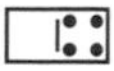 (since the next player can't cover both blanks in one turn), setting up the door to the 4s.

B. Runt

The last player is often the most crucial of all, carrying heavy responsibility for the game strategy. First and foremost, he needs to make the lead player pass. Unless he can do this, the opponents will win.

To make the lead player pass, he needs to develop his strong suit, probably to a greater degree than the 3rd-lead needs to do so. He should attack by repeating and, if possible, squaring to his own strong suit, or to his partner's. This means he will probably pass up more opportunities to play his double tiles. For example:

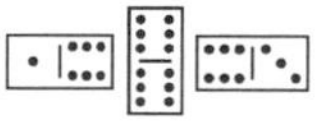

After the leadoff with the 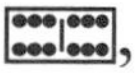, the 2nd-lead played the 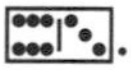. The 3rd-lead played the 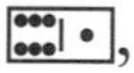, covering his partner's leading suit. Covering his partner's 6 tells us he probably doesn't have any 3s.

The runt may have the  or the 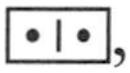, but he shouldn't play either if he has a better tile. If he has the , then he should square to his partner's 3. This is such a straightforward play that, if he doesn't do it, it's assumed he doesn't have the  in his hand. The second-best play he can do is to cover the 3rd-lead's 1 with a strong suit of his own. If he has no 1 tile that he considers strong, he may then double with the .

The , being the double of the partner's strong suit, should be kept for later (see Chapter 11).

The runt should protect his partner against the attack of the lead player. His first play usually covers the leading double:

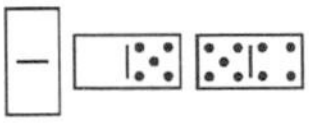

If he has any blanks, then he is expected to play one in order to cover the leadoff 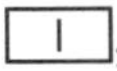, hopefully with a tile that will show his strong suit (and his double, if possible). If his hand has the following tiles:

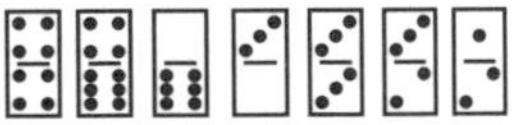

his logical play would be the 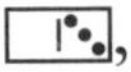, since it both shows his double  as well as his strongest suit. He should *not* double with the 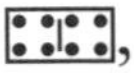, since this may allow the lead player to attack with the blanks (notice the  is missing and could be in the lead player's hand).

We now understand that the runt's main job in this first round is to cover the leadoff tile. This should be done even if the tile he plays is not a particularly strong one. If he doesn't cover it, then we can assume he has none of that suit. *Unless …*

Let's say that after a leadoff with the 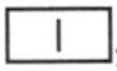, the 2nd-lead thought for a long time before playing the . This tells the runt that he needn't fear his partner will pass to blanks (since the 2nd-lead thought about it, he must have had a choice of tiles) and therefore shouldn't feel forced to cover the leadoff. It even makes him suspicious that the lead player may have led a bluff. In that case the runt should cover the 3rd-lead's tile with the strongest suit he has, attacking the lead player and keeping him off balance.

Just as the 3rd-lead tries to help the lead player develop his game, so should the runt be playing to thwart him. He should play tiles that won't allow the lead player to repeat his strong suit. He should also watch for signals in his partner's plays that tell him to take over the offensive of the game ("pull the hand"). The runt is often in a position to best guess the opponent's tiles, and can therefore win as often as (if not more than) his partner.

Pulling the Hand

The third and fourth positions, the "defensive players," are the most difficult ones to play well. These players are constantly balancing their need to discard bad tiles while developing their strong suits, with a mandate to help their teammates and thwart their opponents. They are the ones often asked to make sacrifices for the sake of their partners, such as not doubling when they can attack instead, or discarding doors they may hold in order to prevent their partners from passing or discarding their doors.

And all the time, like sharks circling bait, they need to be constantly looking for signs of weakness in their partners. To "pull the hand" means that the defensive player has decided his hand is the strongest and in the best position to win. He now plays tiles that benefit the development of his own game *at his partner's expense!*

If you believe your game is best, and are contemplating pulling the hand, keep the following points in mind. Unless your partner has clearly asked you to do so (by the way he's played so far), he is going to immediately feel betrayed. Even if you win, but especially if you lose the hand, you can expect at least some hard feelings on his part. Good manners dictate you should apologize to your partner at the end of the game, and explain why you thought you should play this way.

Here's an example of the runt (last player) pulling the hand:

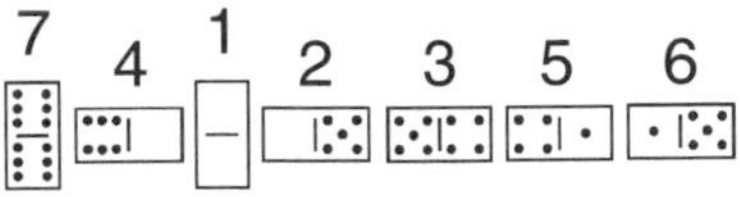

Your partner is 2nd-lead and has played two 5s, the and the . Clearly his strong suit showing is the 5. You have in your hand the . Although you played the first 6, as a supportive player you are expected to play this tile by squaring to 5s.

What would you do, however, if you also have in your hand the   ? If you were to square to 6s, there would be only one 6 missing (the), which someone would have to discard, and you'd keep all the remaining 6s. If you decide to pull the hand you'd play the on your partner's 5 like this:

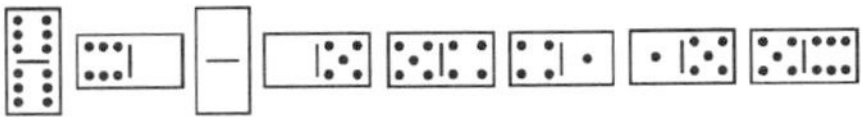

You can also pull the hand by withholding your partner's strong suit, even though you're expected to develop it, simply because another play advances your own hand. This play might even be getting rid of a double tile. All "pulls" somehow involve subordinating your partner's game to yours.

What should you do if you're the partner whose hand has been pulled, even though you didn't want it to happen? If your partner's not prone to these exercises willy-nilly, then you need to trust his judgment. Reexamine the game played so far, in light of this new development. If it's the runt who pulled, he'll take care of making the lead player pass. Your job now is to make the 3rd-lead pass to help the runt take the lead.

If your team loses the game, then expect profuse apologies from the partner who pulled the hand and be sure to scold him, but only good-naturedly!

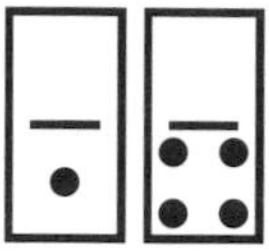

Building a House

So far we've been talking about strategy in a straightforward fashion. Even when pulling the hand, everyone could tell by your plays that you were doing so, and adjusted their strategy accordingly. It's all been very aboveboard and polite.

Now let's get dirty!

There is another way to develop your game that is not immediately obvious to the other players. It is called building a house. I think of it as a passive-aggressive strategy of play. If we compare what we've discussed before to an elegant fencing match, then this is more like mud wrestling: sneaky, controversial, ultimately rather selfish—but you might just win the bout.

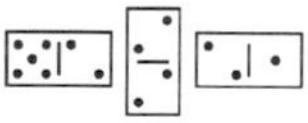

Your leadoff was the  after very little thought (which probably means you have good tiles in your hand—see Chapter 10). 2nd-lead plays the  and your partner rapidly follows with the . This means your partner doesn't have any 1s to play and therefore was forced to cover your leading tile—right? And yet, if we take a look at his hand, this is what we find:

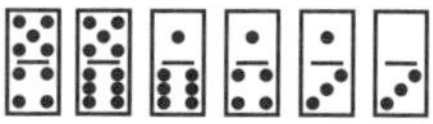

What's going on? Your partner decided that he had strong tiles and pulled the hand by *not* covering the 1.

What's different about this "pull" compared to the ones discussed in the last chapter is that he is being sneaky about it. He needs more 1s, so he's trying to trick the opponents into playing them.

Building a house means you've decided your game isn't strong enough to attack, your partner's not worth supporting or defending, and you're looking for an alternative. So why not let the opponents help your game?

To do this you need to fool everyone else around the table *including your partner*. You must make the opponents believe that you are running away from a particular suit, when in reality you like it very much, in order to get them to develop it for you.

Here's another example. You have the following hand:

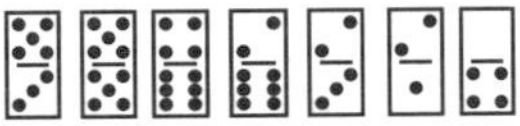

and decide to lead with the .

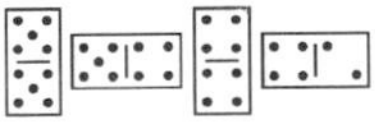

Now you're in a position to cover either your own 5 or the runt's 2. The best reason to leave the 5 alone is because it was your lead suit and your partner expects you to protect it. The 2 was led by your opponent, so covering it with the 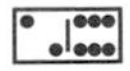 seems to be the right choice.

You have more 2s than 5s in your hand, however. It seems logical to try to develop the 2s. How can you do this? You could think for a while, then play the 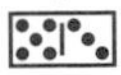 rapidly to indicate you have no other 5s and decided to play with the 2s. Your partner now understands your strategy, but so do the opponents. It's unlikely that the runt will repeat a 2 when he realizes you want to play them.

This may be the right time to build a house. Think before playing the 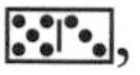, then play it at normal speed. A frown as you think may not be a bad idea. If another player is watching your expressions, he'll surmise that covering your own lead tile is distasteful to you. Everyone will assume you have no 2s, and at least one other 5, and you only grudgingly played the .

Now the fun begins. If your opponents take the bait, they will repeat the 2 as soon as possible and prevent the 5s from being developed—falling right into your trap. Later in the game, when the truth comes out, the opponents will be demoralized as they realize they've been had.

Such a sneaky play is a calculated risk. You can't expect much help from your partner, since he's not clear on what your game is. You now depend upon the opponents' plays. You can't build a house too often, or your opponents will quickly wise up to you. Worse yet, you may lose your partner's support. The common phrase an upset partner exclaims is "I'm playing against two enemies and a traitor!"

And yet ... sometimes you just have to cut loose—go wild—play it *unsafe* and add some spice to your game-playing. Just be prepared to pay the possible consequences.

How to Locate the Unplayed Tiles

Several times in this book there's been a statement like "… if you think the opponent's strong suit is the 5," or "… since your partner has no 3s." How are you supposed to know these things?

Figuring out the tiles in the other players' hands is an advanced skill that requires most of the concepts we've been discussing in the prior chapters. Above all, it requires a keen memory, in order to be able to recall the plays made. I recommend very strongly that you develop this ability to remember by practicing the memory exercises presented in Chapter 5.

For the sake of the subsequent discussion, let's assume you've been playing for a while and have the basic skills down pat. You are now able to reconstruct most of the skeleton as it's been played (who played what tile, and under what circumstances).

You only know *for sure* seven tiles at the beginning of a game: those in your hand. As tiles are played, there will be fewer and fewer unplayed ones to guess, so it becomes easier to figure them out. The goal, which is not always achieved, is to be able to identify them by the time everyone has only two tiles left in his hand.

At the beginning of the game you don't know the other 21 tiles. You will make tentative guesses on what the other players have by the way they play. Remember that you may be playing with others who may not follow your strategy, or just don't know how to play well, so their plays may confuse you. But there is one way you can learn about their tiles that is 100% for certain: their passes.

If a player passes to a certain suit, you can now disregard all seven tiles of that suit from his hand. Eliminating these tiles makes your guessing a lot easier.

Consider the following problem: you led with the 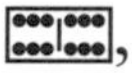, and later passed more than the other players. Now all others have one tile left to play, while you have two. You can play either the  or the . If you knew the other players' tiles, you could make sure your partner wins.

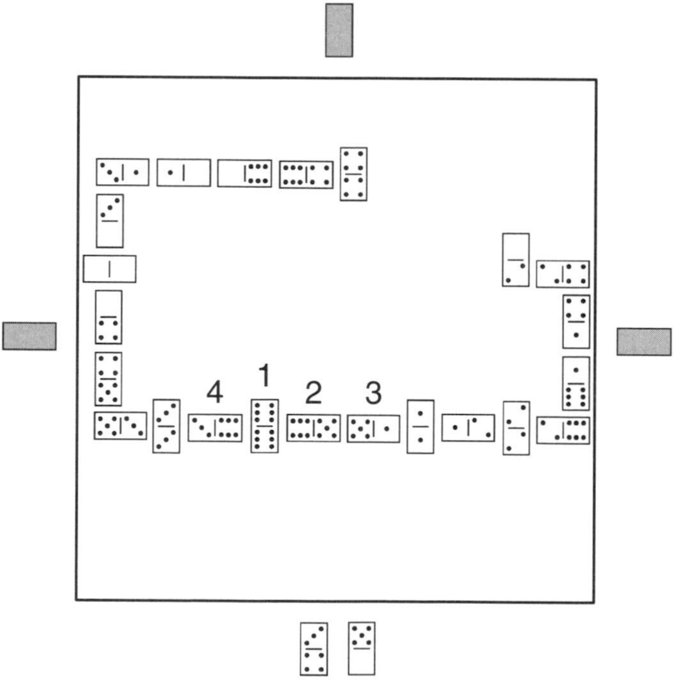

What are the three unplayed mystery tiles? You should be able to tell by studying the skeleton.

Yes, you're correct: they are the , the  and the . If you had to guess, you'd have a one-third chance of guessing right and making the winning play.

You recall the first few tiles played and see that after the 2nd-lead played the , your partner played the 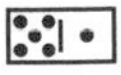; he didn't double on the 5! You should therefore expect him *not* to have the . Good! Now guessing will get you fifty-fifty odds.

But you also realize that the 2nd-lead played as his first tile the 5, and your partner seemed to shy away from it the second time it was played, so the 5 is probably the opponents' strong suit. Although it may still be a guess, your partner probably has the  and you should play the .

If you recall your partner passed to 5s, would that make it any easier? Of course—now you're sure about his tile, since you can identify it as the only non-5, the . Playing the 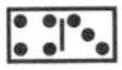 is a guaranteed win.

Apart from the passes, all other ways to figure out the tiles are not as clear-cut. The passes only tell you what the player doesn't have; you'll have to discover what he actually has by the way he plays.

Although the opponents would like to hide their game from you, they must still try to communicate between themselves. If you follow their plays, they often can't help but declare their hands. Here's an example: You're the lead player and you lead with the 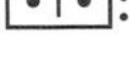:

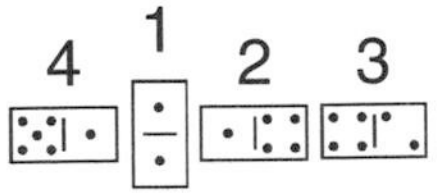

After this round you should know that your partner (3rd-lead) doesn't have the 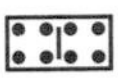 and, since he played the 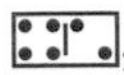, his strong suit might be the 2s.

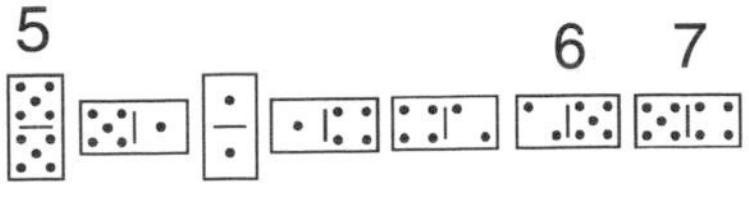

The runt played the 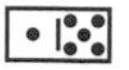 and you doubled up on it. The 2nd-lead squared to his partner's 5 with the 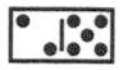 and your partner played the , repeating the opponent's 4. This is not a play you would expect him to make, since you're not supposed to develop the opponent's suit (Second Law). This probably means he has no other 5s.

You also keep in mind that the 2nd-lead didn't like the 2, since he squared against it, so he probably has few or no others. It would seem like a good idea to help your partner develop his 2s.

It's important to figure out the other players' strategies, or styles of play, in order to guess at their tiles. This is not too hard to do if you know the people you're playing with. If they're strangers, however, it'll probably take you a few games into the match before you can figure them out. I make guesses as to their tiles, and then observe what they play. As the game progresses and their tiles get played, I learn what they *really* had in their hands. In this fashion I can determine their skill level and strategy of the game.

Do they play primarily so as not to yield suits? Do they like to build houses? These styles of play make it very difficult to figure out their tiles. That is why sometimes beginner players may defeat an experienced team. Long-term, though, playing in a nonlogical way doesn't lead to consistent victories, since not even your partner can figure out what your hand is and can't help you develop it.

If the opponents are experienced, then I assume that they're playing the best they can with whatever tiles they have, and that they'll be following the Three Laws of Dominotics. I assume that they will first attack, if possible, with their strong suit. Next I assume they'll take any good chance they have to cover, repeat, and square. If they don't do so, then it's either because they're concerned over a double tile, or they just don't have the appropriate tile. Finally, if they cover their own strong suit, or their partner's, then it's because they don't have a tile for the other side of the skeleton—or they have what would be a terrible one to play (the opponent's door, for example).

These assumptions may not be correct, though. The player may not have recognized a key play, and therefore may not have made it. He could also be intentionally trying to confuse you. He may even simply make a mistake in his tile choice.

In summary, when you try to guess the other players' tiles, always think about the following four points:

1) The only tiles you know for sure are those in your own hand.

2) Remember the passes, as this is the only 100% assured knowledge you have about the others' tiles; namely, what they don't have.

3) Determine what strategy of play the others follow.

4) If the others are experienced, then observe the plays they make—and realize the ones they might have done, but didn't. Assume that if they didn't play a particular tile that would have been to their advantage, then it's because they don't have it. You will have the best chance to locate the tiles by eliminating possibilities and by making informed guesses according to those played.

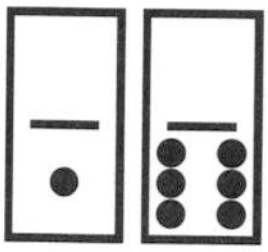

The Jam

The jam is a play that terminates the game being played. It happens when a tile is used to square to a suit so that all seven tiles of that particular suit are played. No further play is therefore possible. The unplayed tiles in each team are then put together and their points are added. The team with the fewest points gets the total points of *both* teams. The second sample game in Chapter 3 ends with a jam.

If the total point sum of one team equals the total of the other team, the jam is deemed a tie and the game is played over. The player who originally led off that game gets to lead off again.

What is the importance of a jam? With this one play you directly control the fate of the game. In one stroke you can win big—or lose big. The stakes are also higher: the points earned are usually more than what you earn when a game ends by discarding the last tile (dominating). This is generally true, even though the most points you can possibly win by dominating is 129, and the highest jam can only give you 126 points.

Psychologically, this play can be a traumatic experience. While the person who has the "jamming tile" (JT) is pondering his choice, all you can do is wait and hope he'll make the decision that will benefit you. You also try to develop a poker face so he won't see your barely suppressed joy (or dread) at the thought of the coming jam.

This play is sometimes the only way out of a hopeless situation. You may have a hung double tile and can't win by dominating—but still might win by jamming the game (a [|] or a [•|•] are great tiles to have in a jam). You may even be about to lose the game and are desperately hoping a jam will result in a tie, thus giving you an opportunity to play the game over without a penalty.

How can you tell if a jam is a right choice to make? The first task you have to do is to figure out how many points are unplayed. You add the points of the tiles played (*including* the points of the JT about to be played) and subtract them from 168 (the total number of points of all 28 tiles). Then you may follow this decision tree:

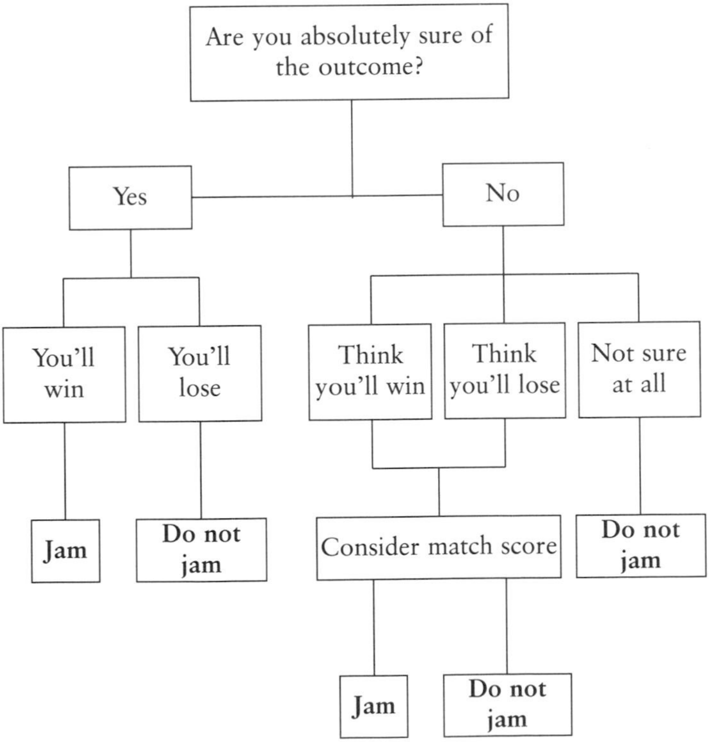

The first decision branch in this tree is to determine if you can be absolutely sure you'll win or lose the jam. How is this possible? Observe this example:

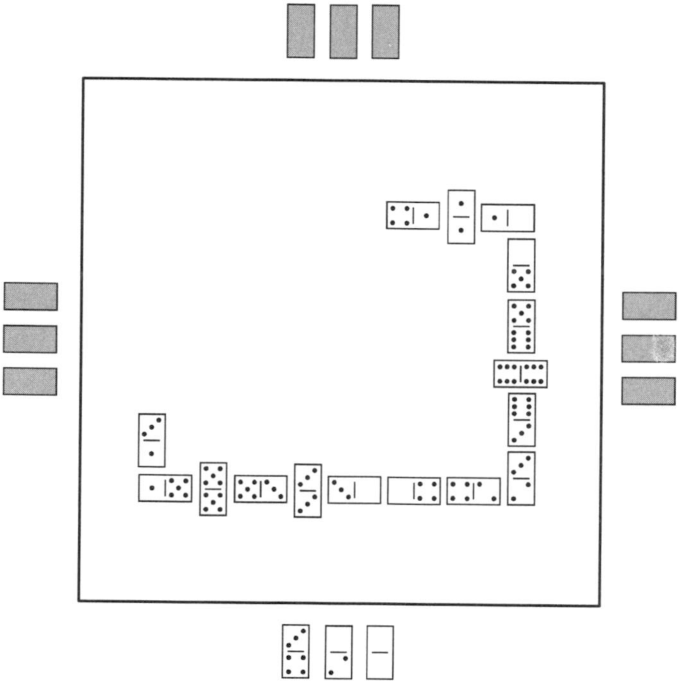

You have the jamming tile (JT), the . First you add all the played points, which equal 97. Add those of the JT and you have a total of 104. Now subtract 168 – 104 = 64 points in the unplayed tiles. This means if you and your teammate have total points less than 32, you win the jam.

Your own tiles (after you play the JT) add up to 2 points. Now assuming your partner has the three heaviest tiles (the ones worth the most points), how much would he have? The three unplayed tiles with the most points are 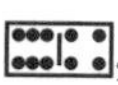, 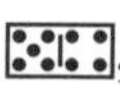, and 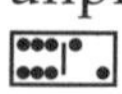 (tied with 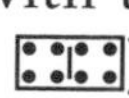), which total 27. If you now add your own points, you see your team can have *at most* 29 points. This is a jam you can't lose. Play the  on the .

For another result, consider this example:

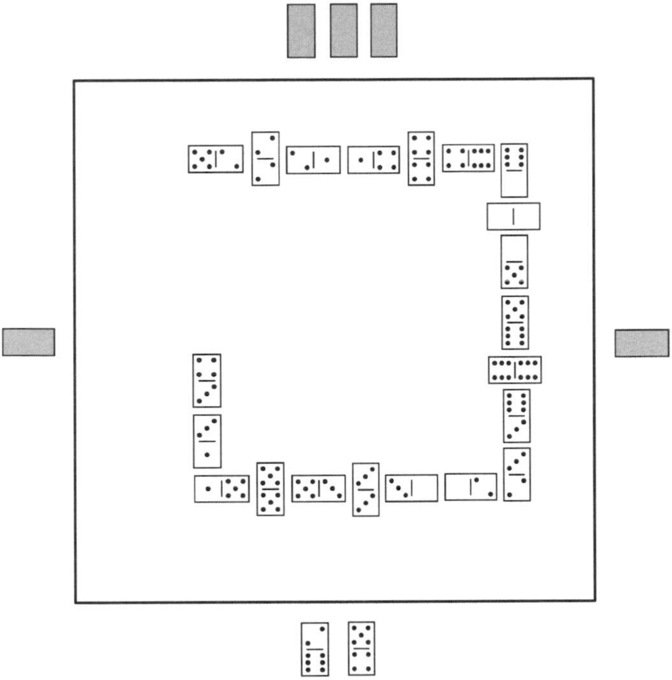

Now your jamming tile is the . The total of played points, *including* the JT, is 140. There are therefore 28 points unplayed, and 14 are needed for a tie. If you assume your partner has the three lightest tiles, the 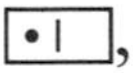, the , and the 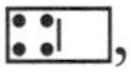, he would have 7 points. This, added to your 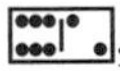, is 15 points. Since the fewest number of points your team can have is more than half of the unplayed points, you can't win the jam. So play the  on the 5 and let the game continue.

As you've seen, adding up the points can give you critical information, so it's important to be accurate in your calculations. This is a good time to give you a hint: in a jamming situation, the total of the unplayed points (after you play the JT) *must always be an even number.*

If your calculations give you an odd number, then you've made an error; go back and add again.

The next branch in the decision tree to consider is what to do if you can't be absolutely sure you'll win the jam. You may have one of three impressions: you suspect your team has fewer points and will therefore win, you suspect your team will lose, or you have no idea who will win.

Perhaps the easiest one to deal with is what to do if you have no idea at all. Usually this is because the jam has come early in the game, before you've had a chance to figure out the other players' tiles. This also means there are probably a lot of points out there to be won—or lost! Jamming the game in this situation is pure gambling, and you must decide if you're a gambler at heart or not. I usually don't jam when faced with this situation.

It is difficult to know what to do when you're somewhere in between being certain of the outcome of a jam and having no idea at all, but this is actually the most common situation you'll find yourself in. By then, you've begun to guess the other players' tiles and have a fighting chance of predicting the outcome. Consider the example on the next page.

The JT is the 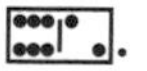. Now the total of unplayed points is 44, and there is no 100% assurance of either losing or winning. I'll let you do the calculations, but your team can have a maximum of 26 points (more than half of points left—you lose) or a minimum of 14 (you win).

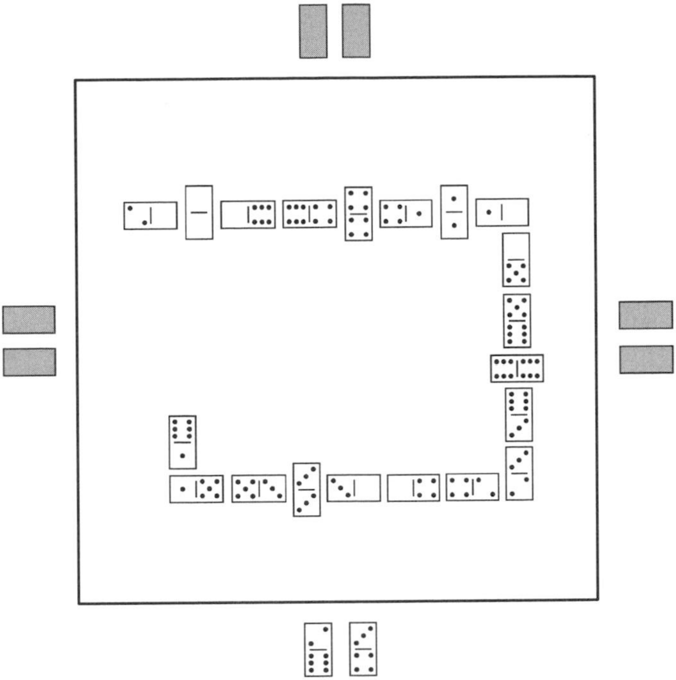

It might seem like the outcome is now left to chance, until you remember (in this sample game) that the opponents were playing the 5s as their strong suit. Your partner didn't double on the 5, but rather covered it, so he probably doesn't have the . Assume therefore he has only one 5, the heaviest one being the . Now assume his other tile is the heaviest *non*-5 left (the  or the 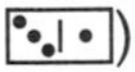), and when you add his 13 to your 7 points, you get only 20 points. You should win the jam, 20 points to 24.

Otherwise, if it's your partner who has been playing the 5s, then assume he has two of the three left. If he has the two lightest ones, he has a total of 16 points (the 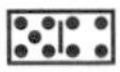 and the ), and with your 7 you get 23 and you lose the jam.

There will still be situations where you may not know

the right choice to make. You may think you'll win, but can't be sure, and worry about the consequences that losing the jam will have on the match. This is when I recommend figuring the match score into your calculations.

You will probably feel more brave and jam the game if it's early in the match, or if the opponents have few total points. This way, if you lose, you still have plenty of opportunities to make up for your mistake. You will, however, be reluctant to jam if all they need to win are the points at stake. It's better in that case to open the game and dump points, hoping to win the next game.

Sometimes your partner can give you a hint that he thinks a jam would be good, and this hint may tip the scales one way or the other. You may see your partner think long and hard when he knows you have the JT, and then very deliberately play a tile so you get a chance to jam the game. This means he has studied his hand, determined it's not too heavy, and wants to give you the signal that it's okay by him to jam. This is called "asking for the jam." Now you can study your own tiles and let them make the decision for you.

It's been said that it's not wise to jam a game that's already won. On the next page is an example.

You have the , but this time you also have another 2 and are therefore not obligated to play the JT. When you add the points and calculate, you realize that the outcome is not absolutely known (if your partner has heavy tiles, you lose the jam). You also realize that if you play the 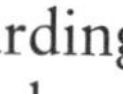, then no one can stop you from winning by discarding the  in the next turn because *you* are the lead player at this point. Why then run the risk of jamming the game?

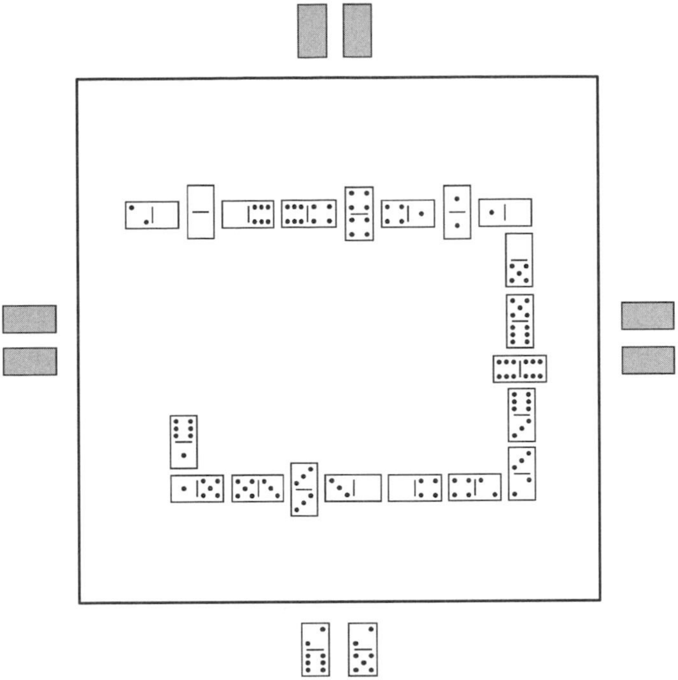

This reasoning is a sound one *if* you're not sure who would win the jam, or if you think you'd lose it. If you're pretty sure you'd win it, however, then *not* jamming is foolish. All you're doing is allowing the opponents to discard tiles, whose points would have been added to your team score.

Even with a won game, therefore, seriously study the possibility of the jam. It may be worth it.

What if you don't jam the game? Perhaps you have another tile that can play instead of the JT (as in the last example), and may therefore keep the door for at least one more round. If you don't have such a tile then your only other choice is to square to the other number.

If I'm your partner and I see you do this, then I should understand that you were afraid of losing the jam. Is this because you think I have heavy tiles, or are *you* the one who's loaded with points? The answer to this question will tell me a lot about your hand. It is unlikely you have any others of the suit you squared to; otherwise you would have played another tile and kept the JT.

Talking about the jam can be an exhaustive task—and yet there may always remain an element of uncertainty in your decision of whether to do it or not. Unless the outcome is a sure thing, the jam will always remain, in a sense, a calculated gamble, a gamble that may significantly advance your game—or sink it!

The Three Doors (and Other Stories)

In this chapter I've collected a few plays and situations that couldn't be clearly pigeon-holed into one category or another. Let's discuss them one at a time.

I. The Three Doors

Let's say that a square has happened so you are left holding the last two doors and the double. For example:

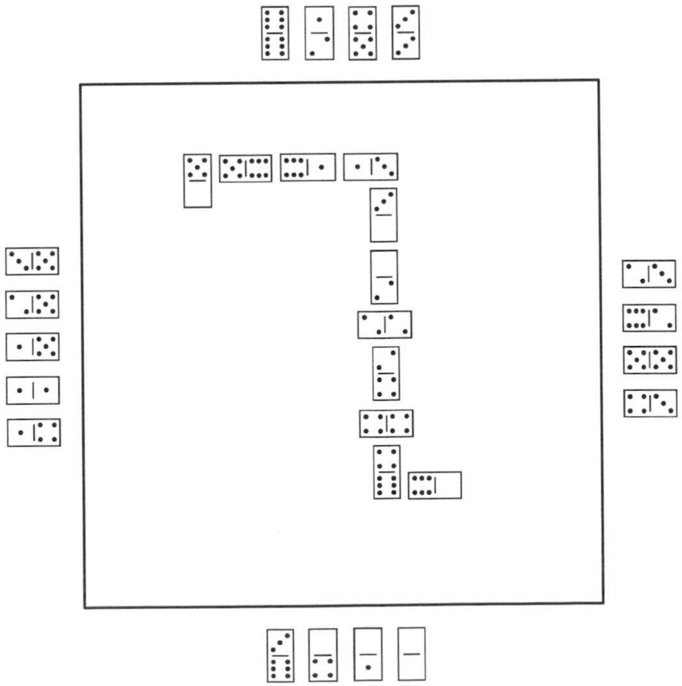

You're the lead player now. What could be easier than to double with the 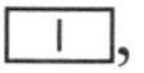, make everyone pass, and then play either door?

As in this example, it often happens that after you follow up with one of the doors, on the next round you'll have to discard the last one and you'll lose the game! Try to play either the 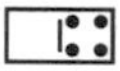 or the 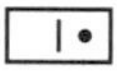 and you'll see what I mean.

It is therefore better to hold on to that double. This way, when the runt plays the  or the  (depending on which blank you play) you'll be able to double with the 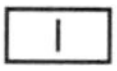 and still hold on to the door. When your partner sees you play your double, he'll knows what suit you don't have and will try to protect you from it.

Keeping the double tile effectively gives you two doors in a row. So why would you ever want to play the double? I can think of only one good reason: if your three doors are your last three tiles. In that case, play the 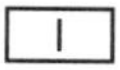 to make everyone pass and proceed to dominate the game.

II. The Open Tile

Your partner has just led with an open tile; that is, a tile that has a different suit on each side and is therefore not a double. There are several different strategies to follow, according to what you think is going on.

A. Almodovar's Opening

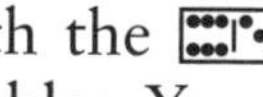

Your partner leads with the 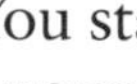 and you observe you have neither of the doubles. You start suspecting he used Almodovar's Opening. If so, your partner probably has a poor game with many doubles, and led with an open tile whose suit's doubles are in his hand (he has the  and the ). When the 2nd-lead doesn't double either, then it's almost assured your assessment is correct, since it's unlikely the runt has both doubles.

What you should do is immediately square to the 6, since this will help your partner play the . If you don't do so, it's assumed you don't have the .

B. The 2nd-Lead Doubles

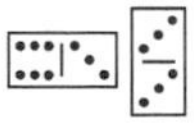

You immediately know this is not Almodovar's, since the 2nd-lead played a double. You may even have the other double in your hand. What should you play?

If you have the 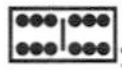, then this should be the obligatory play. With it, you won't be covering either of the lead-off suits, and you force the runt to play a fresh suit to your partner, who may then have the chance to square.

If you don't have the , then you need to play to cover the 6, so your partner knows you *don't* have the double and may therefore hang it if the opportunity presents itself.

C. The 2nd-Lead Covers and You Have a Double

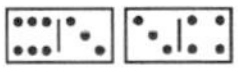

You have the 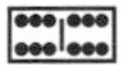 or the , so you know this is not Almodovar's. You also may even have the . What you *don't* want to do in this situation is to play a double, since it's possible that the runt may have the  and square to 4, perhaps making your partner pass and lose the lead. You would think for a while (if you have other 4s) then cover the 4 with an open tile. This keeps your partner out of trouble.

D. The Lead Player Has One of the Doubles

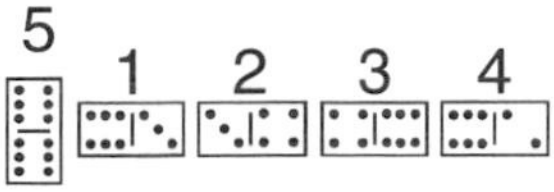

Let's say you have the , so you know it's not Almodovar's. Yet on his next play, your partner doubles to the 6!

This means he felt secure enough his 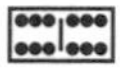 wouldn't be hung even if he led with the open tile—therefore he must have started with five or six 6s in his hand. Now you need to play in order to let him develop that monster suit.

It also tells us he has no 2s, otherwise he would have kept that  in his hand.

III. The Ill-Repeat

As a corollary to cover, repeat, and square, there is a particular play that should be admonished: as a general rule, you should not repeat the opponent's suit.

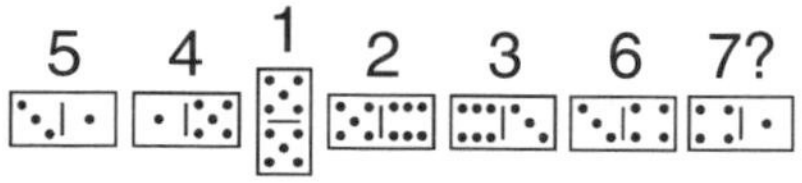

In this example you're the 3rd-lead. In the second round, rather than cover the 3 you played first, you played the . This helps to develop the opponent's suit (which is against the Second Law). At best, it may allow the opponent to double on the tile. At worst, being the third of that suit played, a square will give him the door(s).

It is therefore better to play something else rather than to repeat their suit. You may need to cover your partner's tile, or even your own, rather than assist in the development of the opponents' suit.

Perhaps the only time when the ill-repeat wouldn't be quite so dangerous is if you hold a door on the other side of the skeleton, and therefore know for certain that the opponents will have to cover the suit you play.

IV. The Crossed Tiles

Let's say that during a game it becomes obvious that your team has a particular suit. One opponent may have passed to it and the other may have been forced to cover his own strong suit, or even thrown away a door. These are all clear signs that you and your partner have all the tiles left in that suit. For example:

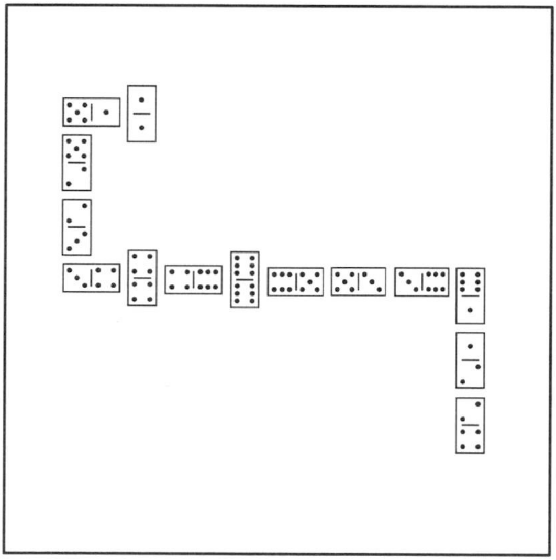

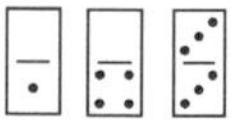

Your team's strong suit is the 1s. You have in your hand one of them, the ; you also have a 4, the . You know for sure your partner has the other two 1s, the  and the . What do you play?

The answer would be very straightforward if you could square to the 1s, but you don't have the . Your first instinct might therefore be to leave the 1 alone, and cover the 4 with the . Otherwise you'll be covering your strong suit, and may make your partner believe you have no 4s to play.

However, it often happens that whatever you play on the 4 can be used by your next opponent to attack your partner; he then has to cover the 1 with one of his tiles, such as the . This leaves each of you with one 1 in your hand and, because you *didn't* square to 1, the  is now known to be in your partner's hand.

Having crossed tiles (one in each teammate's hand) is troublesome. The opponents can now play their tiles so that neither of you can play the 1; they'll play blanks to him, and 4s to you. It's often therefore much more powerful to cover the 1 with the 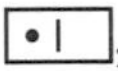, but *only* if you're sure your partner has the other two 1s.

Consider thinking for a while before playing the . Your partner, who knows you have only one 1, should understand you do have a 4, but decided not to cross the strong suit. The opponents may be fooled into thinking not only that you have no 4s, but also that you have other 1s. They won't expect your partner to have both of them, and this may even allow a jam to be set up since they may not expect him to have the JT.

As an aside, what if you did have the  in your hand? You should square to 1s, make the opponent pass, and your partner should then play his tile *rapidly*. He won't fool you, since you know he has the door, but the opponents may be tricked into thinking you have it—and inadvertently allow your partner to jam the game.

V. The Last Door

Your partner has just now been forced to discard his door, and never had a chance to contemplate a jam. Now it's your turn to play and you're desperately trying to figure out what his remaining tile is—but you have *absolutely no idea!* What do you do?

I always depend on figuring out the tiles, rather than relying on luck or hunches. But there's a "rule" that has helped me often in this situation. Consider this:

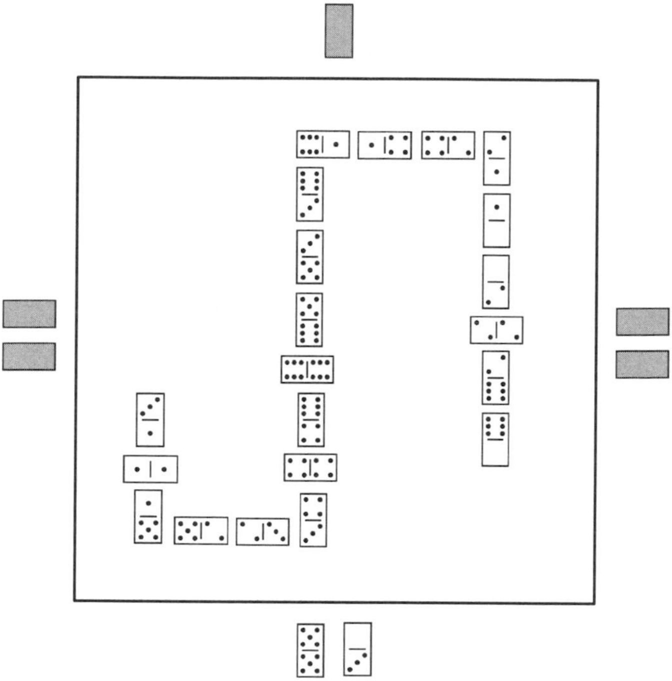

The door your partner played was the 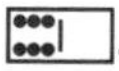. If he had been presented with a blank before, he would have attacked with the 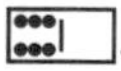. He may have even considered jamming the game, if it happened to be the jamming tile. This means he was most likely never given the chance to play a blank—and therefore it is likely he has another blank in his hand.

You can reconstruct the skeleton in your mind (you've been practicing, haven't you?), and can determine for a fact if your partner did indeed have a chance to play a blank. When you don't know for sure what your partner's tile is, and feel the need to guess, look at the other suit on the door he just discarded and assume he has one of those left. In this case, squaring to blank with the 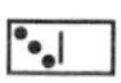 may be your best chance to win this game, since now there's a blank on either end of the skeleton, assuring one for your partner.

VI. The Penultimate Sacrifice

If the ultimate sacrifice is to hang your own double to benefit your partner, then the penultimate one must be to throw away your door when you're not forced to. The sacrificial player is the one that has more tiles, trying to prevent his leading partner from passing.

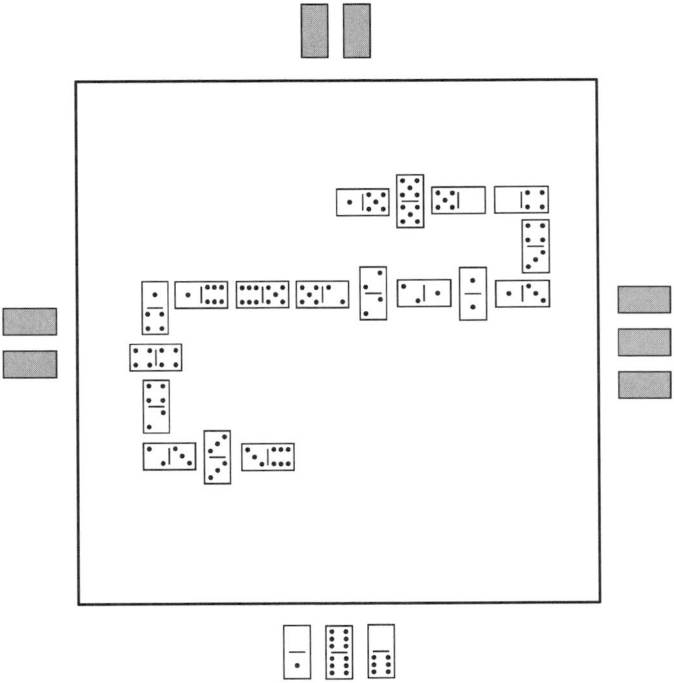

It's your turn, and what could be more clear-cut that your need to double with the 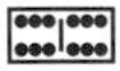? After all, you discard a bad tile and still retain the door to the 1s. You fleetingly remember your partner led with the 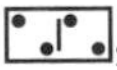, but fail to grasp that clue's significance. So you play the 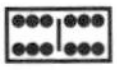 and promptly proceed to lose the game. What happened? Here's how the tiles were actually distributed:

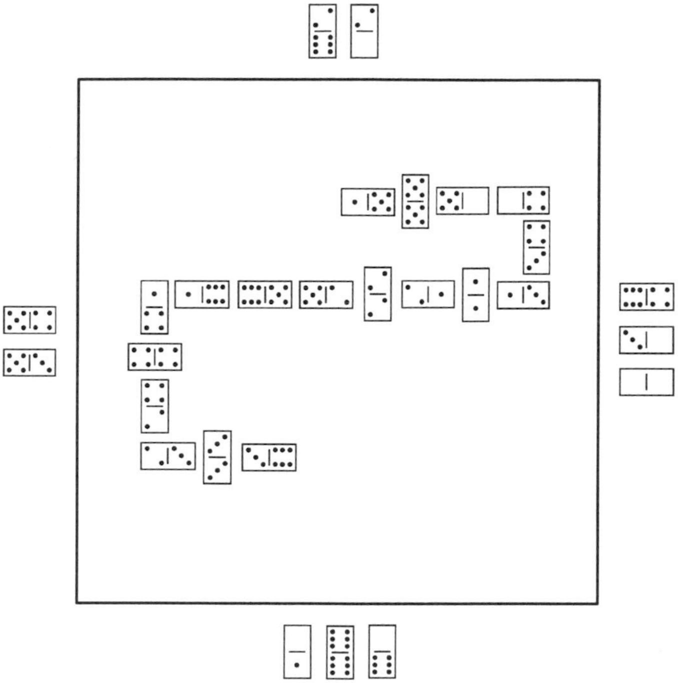

If you'd been following the game and trying to guess the tiles as you went along, then this shouldn't have been a surprise to you. Any play other than to sacrifice your door causes your partner to pass and the opponents to win.

Your partner led with the and played to develop this suit. Observing that the two 2s left were the and the , you realize that playing the door ensures one of them can be played and opens up the game for your partner. You should think before playing it, though, so he realizes you weren't forced into it and therefore still had another play option.

VII. Man Overboard!

The lead player leads with the and your partner

passes right off the bat. The 3rd-lead plays the 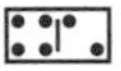 and it's your turn to play the runt position. If you have options on both sides of the skeleton, what do you do now? Do you cover the 4 to help your partner (throw a line to the man overboard)? Or, since he already passed, do you hoard the 4 in your hand to have when you're next attacked with it (let him sink or swim)?

These are the facts: 1) You need to make both the lead player and the 3rd-lead pass if you hope to win; and 2) you need your partner's help to do this. How can he make an opponent pass when he's drowning against the 4s? Let's look at the different possibilities.

If you have the double of the tile shown by the 3rd-lead (in this example the 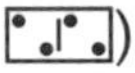), then you should play it. You get rid of a double and you force the lead player to cover either his partner's or his own suit. Either way, your partner should be able to play on his next turn.

If you don't have that particular double and you have one or two 4s, then you should cover the 4. This ensures that the lead player can't repeat the 4 and your partner should be able to play.

What if you have three or four 4s—should you sneakily leave the  alone in order to build a house and try to win with them? It is sometimes said, "He who plays with the lead amuses himself but doesn't win!" Unless you have an overwhelming group of tiles, it's still better to cover the 4 and help your partner.

What if you have only one 4—and the other side of the tile is also the only one of its suit? For example, your only 4 is the —and it's also the only 5 you have. Playing it might be counterproductive, since you yield both suits in one fell swoop. You may also make your partner wrongly believe that the 5s are your strong suit, and he might play to develop them. On the other hand, keeping this tile is very dangerous because you may be forced to play it on a 5. It's best to throw a line to the man overboard. Play the  quickly, so your partner knows it's the only 4 you have, and he might therefore be suspicious of the 5s.

If you have *five* 4s in your hand, though ... beware everyone. You're pulling this hand!

VIII. The Betrayal

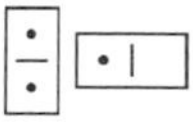

You are the 3rd-lead and you have these tiles:

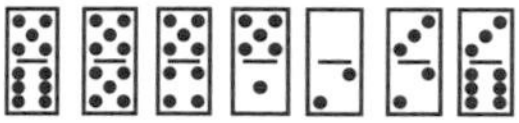

The standard play is to cover the opponent's blank with the 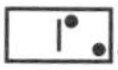. Some influential players have advocated the  (covering your partner's leadoff tile) as a reasonable alternative play. Let's see if we can understand why.

Both of the tiles already played are low in points. There's a chance your partner might be thinking of jamming the game if he's playing the 1s, and he must somehow find out you are loaded with points. Playing the  shows the 5s as your strong suit, as well as the double in your hand, and begins to discard points. If your partner helps you by repeating the 5 (as he should) you are now in a very strong position to dominate the game. If you also happen to jam with your 5s, the 1s in your partner's hand are now an asset.

Remember to think before *rapidly* playing the . This will clearly tell your partner you do have a blank but chose not to use it, and that this was your only 1. You now hope the betrayal will be understood for the smart play it can be.

Sample Games

The final chapter presents four sample games that illustrate the concepts taught throughout the book. These games are seen exclusively from my point of view; you won't know what the other players' tiles are until they lay them down. I believe this will be most instructive in demonstrating the concepts discussed.

My playing technique is similar to that of chess: there are only a limited number of plays possible, which I constantly try to anticipate. While the players think, I ask myself what will be the tile played and what will be the consequences following its play. If I think far enough ahead, then I'll know what my best play should be when my turn comes up. In this way I'll be able to play fast or slow (in order to use thinking to communicate with my partner) without having to waste time and possibly confuse my partner.

I start each game by analyzing my hand and deciding what will be my initial strategy (offensive, defensive, or supportive). Next I try to figure out the other players' strategies as well as their strengths and weaknesses, according to the tiles played. I keep track of the doubles and make guesses about the location of unplayed tiles. The Three Laws of Dominotics are always kept in mind.

To get the most out of these examples you should follow along with your domino set. Start by separating the seven tiles I begin with, and leave the rest in a separate pool from which you will draw as needed to build the skeleton. After each game is done, you should be able to figure out the tiles that the other players started with. You may wish to distribute them and replay the game to better follow my observations and suggestions. I will be the South player, playing with North against East-West.

Game in Which I Play the Lead Player Position
My hand is this:

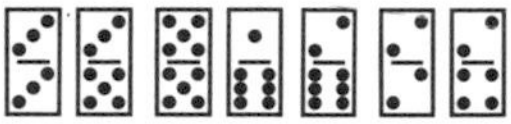

It is a poor hand because I have three doubles and no blanks. Since I have more than two doubles, I look for a tile that would allow me to lead off with Almodovar's Opening. I find the 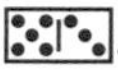. To review this leadoff refer back to Chapter 7.

After thinking for a while (letting my partner know I'm having trouble deciding what to play) I lead with the . East thinks for a while, then plays the . By now my partner has figured out why I led with the , and assumes I have the  and . My partner squares to 5 with the 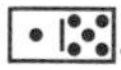. It's a good play because he's repeating the 5 and allows me to double.

West thinks a disturbingly long time (he has many 5s), then plays the . This is the skeleton so far:

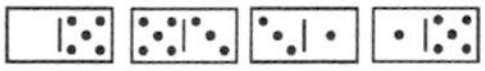

Here's the blank I was dreading! At least I get to play my 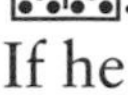. East also thinks for a while, then plays the 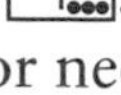. If he covers his partner's blank he either has no 5s or needs to develop the 6s. My partner plays the 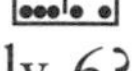 without thinking about it too much. Is that his only 6? Apparently he doesn't have the 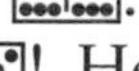. Surprisingly, West then squares to 5 with the 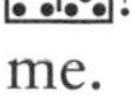! He's trying to wrest control of the 5s away from me.

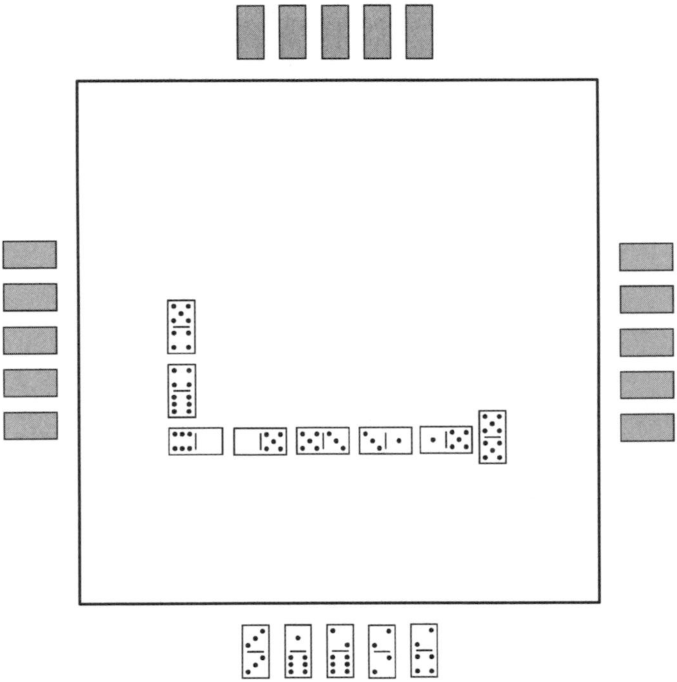

I pass—but so do East and North! This is called a general pass and the two remaining 5s are in West's hand. West has now gone from last position to first, from runt to lead player. He smiles, then plays the , repeating his partner's 6.

Now I have a choice on the 6s. I won't play the 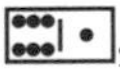, because then I'd be repeating the 1 that East played first. I therefore play the 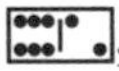, 2s being my strongest suit. East rapidly plays the  (no other 2s?). My partner again thinks on the 1 and, after deliberating, doubles with the . West plays the 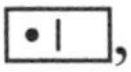, repeating his blank.

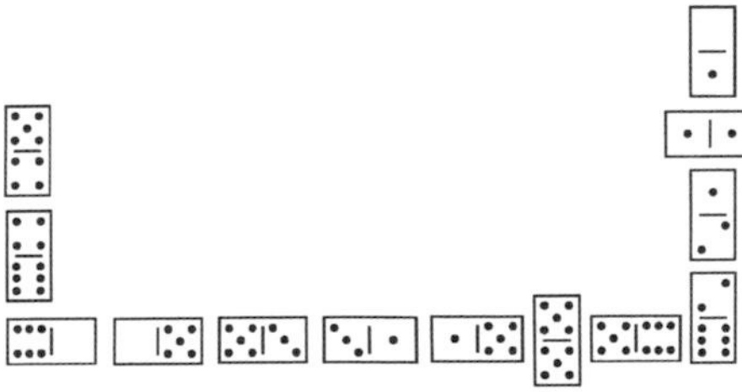

I pass. Couldn't my partner have prevented the blank from being repeated? Since I have the 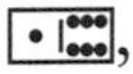, the other 1 left (which must be in North's hand, since he thought on it) is the , and the  is also unplayed. A blank may have been unavoidable.

Now East stops and thinks for a while. Can we figure out what his blanks are? It's not the 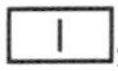, or he would have doubled as his second move. It shouldn't be the 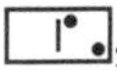, since he played his 2 last turn rapidly. This leaves us with the 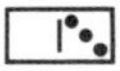 and the 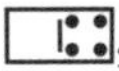, and we understand his dilemma.

He doesn't want to play the 3, since it's my leadoff. He's unhappy about the 4 because my partner played one already. He finally decides to play the 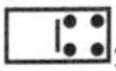, perhaps as the lesser of two evils.

Now my partner thinks a relatively long time (he has a choice of 4s), then doubles with the  ... and West loses his door to the 5s!

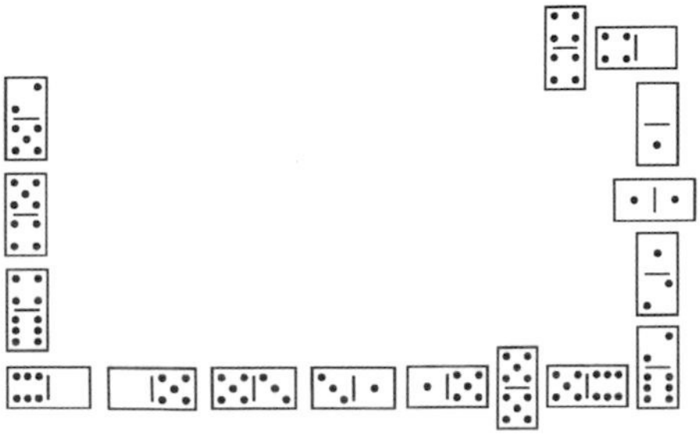

My partner is strong in 4s. I have the  and I square to 4. East passes! My partner (North) now thinks for a short while, then plays the to repeat my lead-off. He well knows that I have the . West passes (no 3s and my partner has the door to 4s), and North becomes the lead player.

Now I get to play my . East thinks about it briefly, then plays the , repeating his 6. My partner indeed has to discard his door, the . West passes again.

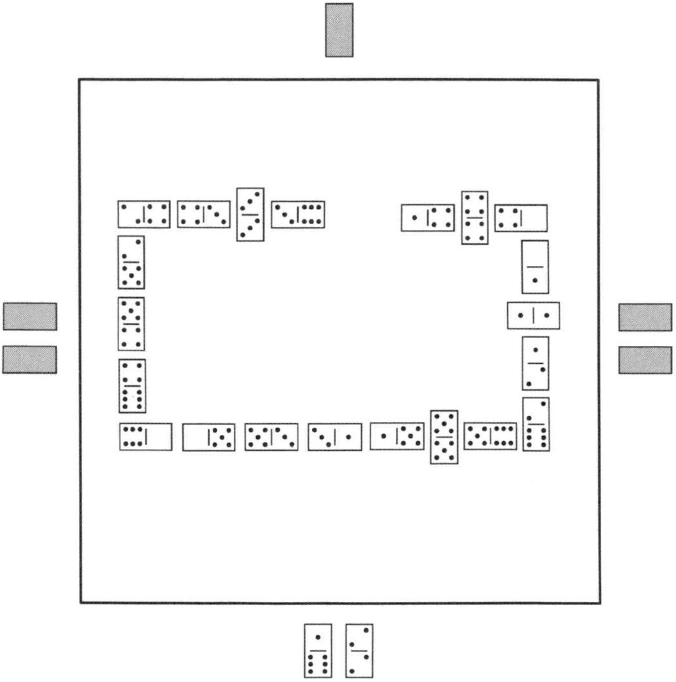

Now I have the choice of either jamming the game to 1, hanging the , or squaring to 6 and letting East jam. Do you agree that East has the ? There should be no doubt about that. West just passed to 6 and North threw away his door to 4s because of the 6.

Can I win the jam to 1? After jamming there will be 142 points played, so 26 points are still unplayed. Half of that is 13, so we win if the opponents have more than that. The three smallest unplayed tiles are the , the , and the . Added to the , this makes a *minimum* possible of 17 points for East-West, so this is a jam I cannot lose!

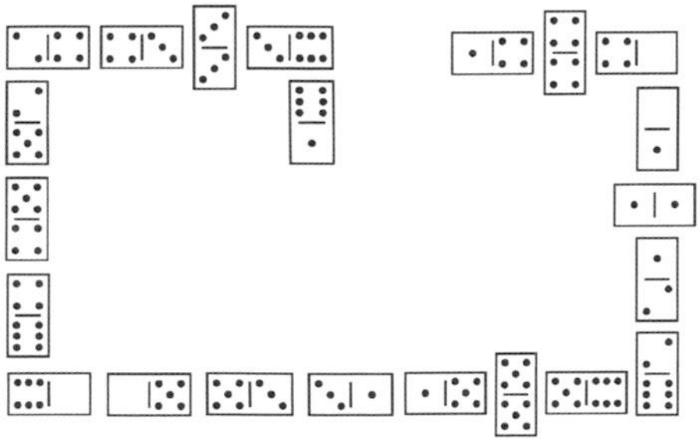

East had the along with the , while North had the . Our team wins the jam's 26 points.

Game in Which I Play the 2nd-Lead (West Leads)

My hand is this:

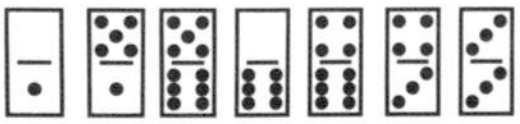

It is an average hand, lacking 2s and having one double with another of its suit. The 6s are my strongest suit with three of them. I'm already worrying that West may lead with the , because then I'll pass immediately.

The leadoff, however, is the . This means either a terrific hand for West (no doubles) or perhaps an Almodovar's Opening, since I don't have either double. I play the , to show my partner my best suit. East squares to 2 with the . North, my partner, passes.

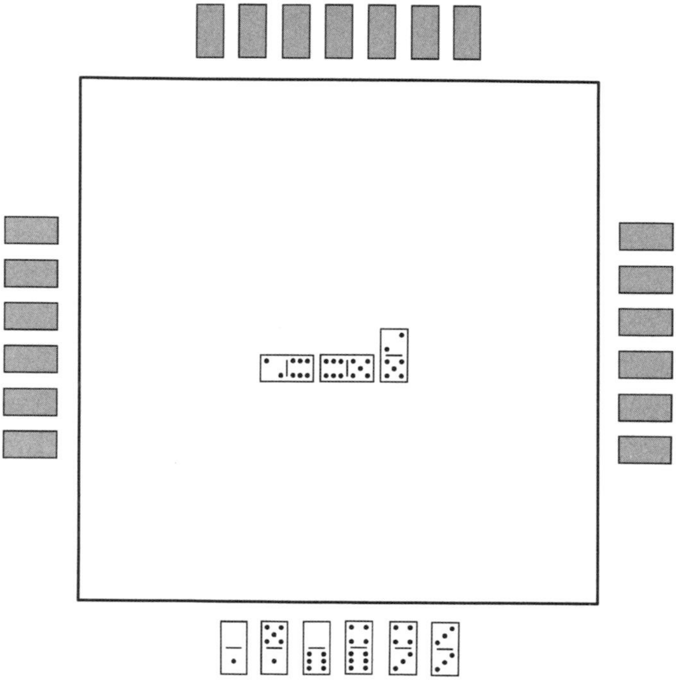

Disaster! The opponents have all the 2s! And now, if West has the 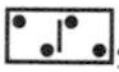, he will play it and make me pass. If he does have it, then it's likely he started with five 2s in his hand. He plays the , however. That means I've now located the 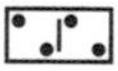 in East's hand.

I can now play the  or the . If I play the double, then the next player can't square to 2 and therefore my partner should be able to play. The 2s, however, are unstoppable, and if we're going to have a chance of winning this game then they must be spent quickly. The  may be a better play. Besides, the  may not be in East's hand, and this way I'd locate another tile. Even if East squares to 2 and my partner passes again, West would still be unable to make me pass. I therefore play the .

East had the right tile after all and plays the 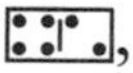, making my partner pass again.

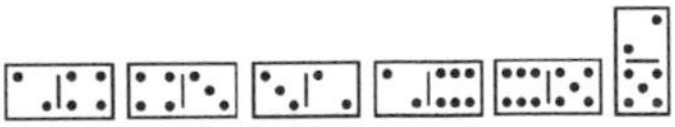

West has to cover another of his 2s and therefore can't threaten me. He thinks for a short time, then plays the . If he thought about it, then he probably has the other 2 in his hand, the 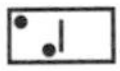.

Now my choices are the  or the 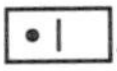. I've already figured out the 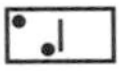 is in West's hand, so if I play the blank, East can't square to 2s again. If I play the 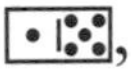, then I'm playing the other lead suit, helping to develop the 5s. The choice is clear: I'll play the 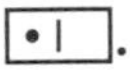.

Consider that if West thought on the 2 without having any others, then East has the 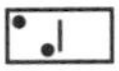 and I've fallen into a trap, giving him the chance to jam the game, which would be a huge loss for my team.

East rapidly plays the 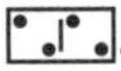. He not only doesn't have the door of the 2s, he probably has no blanks in his hand.

Now it's North's first chance to play. He thinks for a while, so he has other blanks. The best play to make is the 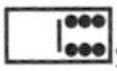, to repeat my 6, but I have that tile. A bad play would be to double on the blank (allowing a jam) or play a 5 (which West led). A 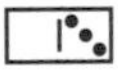 or 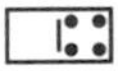 would be a good tile, if he has either of them. He plays the 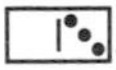.

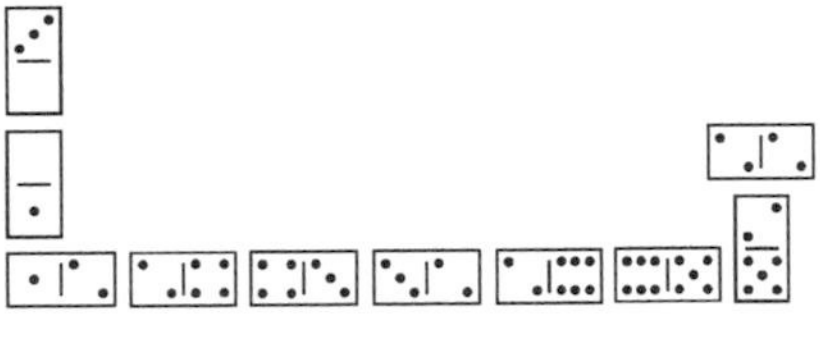

West, still the lead player, plays the . This is a good play since he repeats his other lead suit, the 5s.

My play is forced: the . East plays the , clearing his double.

The best play for North now to make would be to repeat the 3, if he has the . This would not only be a repeat to West, it might allow me to play my . Of course, he doesn't know who has the , just that West doesn't have it (he would have led the game with it, or played it in the last round). He thinks for a short while, then plays the . Is it because he doesn't have the ? After all, the  is missing and East might attack with it. Does my partner have the  and therefore know West can't play it? Or was he simply trying to repeat the 4, which was my second tile played?

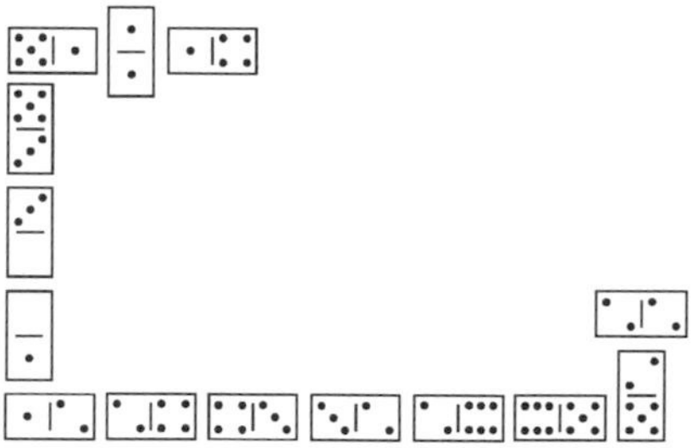

West now doubles with the 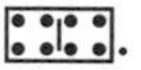. If he led the game with an open tile, then this means he probably has no other 4s. This is critical information. He now has two tiles left and we know one is the 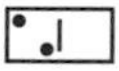 and the other one is *not* a 4. This other tile could be a 6 or a blank but if it's a 5 (his other lead suit), then it has to be the 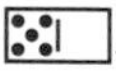. I have now tentatively guessed his remaining tiles.

Although my play is forced, the  is still a strong play. I'm repeating the 6 that I started with, and the 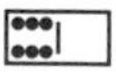 is in my hand so West won't get the blank he needs to jam the game.

East rapidly plays the 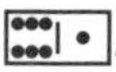. He doesn't have the 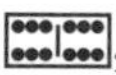, which must therefore be in the hand of my partner, and by the quickness of his play it seems like he has no other 6s.

North plays the 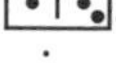. He did have it after all! I wish he had played it during his last turn.

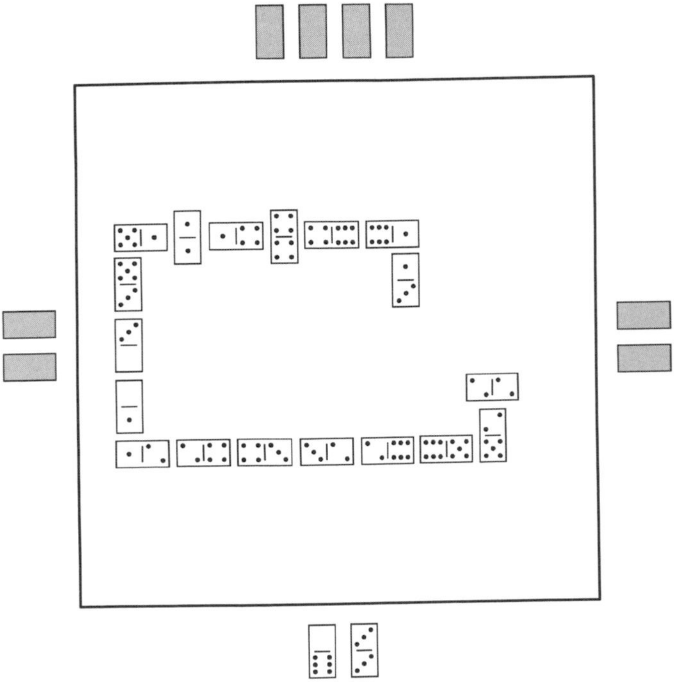

Can we figure out the tiles in the other players' hands? Let's start with East. We already know he has no blanks, and if we also eliminate the 6s, then the only two tiles left are the  and the . West has the door of the 2 and, I think, the . This is purely a guess, though. In that case my partner must have the 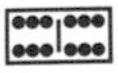 and the 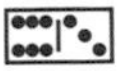 in his hand, as well as the 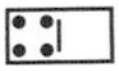 and the 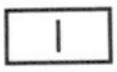.

Now I've tentatively figured out everyone's tiles using the observations and assumptions made throughout the entire game. Let's see if the subsequent plays prove me right. To begin with, West shouldn't have a 3 and he should be forced to discard his door. Sure enough, he plays the 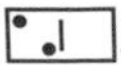. The 2s are finally dead.

My  is in danger of getting hung, but what would happen if I doubled with it? East would pass (no 3s or blanks). North would then need to make a decision.

Should he play his in order to send me the 6 that I need? This would leave the blank open and I think that West has a blank and would win. The same would happen if my partner doubled with the . If he covered the blank with the then both West and I would pass, but East would play the , and West would win with his .

My other choice would be to play the , sending the 6s to my partner. East would pass and my partner should realize that I have the (and *not* hang it). The best play to make then would be to hang his own by squaring to 3, giving me the win and keeping the to count as points for us. Will he understand what I'm trying to do?

I play the , and East passes. North, not being too sure of himself, decides to play the , keeping the door of the 6s—not the best play, but at least he doesn't hang my 3.

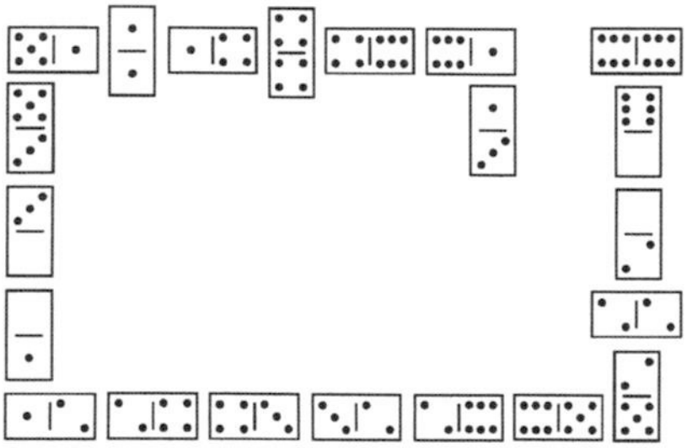

West passes! I win by playing my last tile, the . Here's how the table looked at the end of the game:

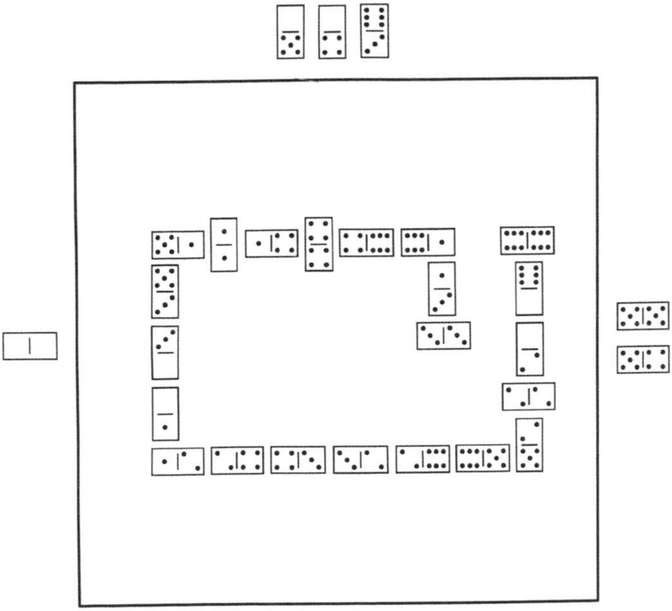

It turned out that West had the , so although he did have a blank, I erred in the specific guess. Thankfully, it wasn't a critical mistake and the game played out to our advantage. Our team wins 37 points.

Game in Which I Play the 3rd-Lead (North Leads)
My hand is this:

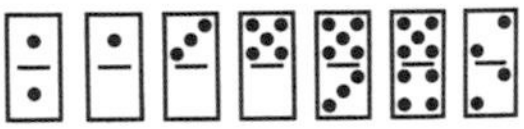

It has no 6s and the only 2 is a double. I hope to combine either the 5s or the blanks with my partner.

North leads with the . West quickly follows with the . Since I have no 6s I must cover my partner's lead tile, and I play the quickly to let him know I have no other 4s either. If East has the , then I would expect him to use it now. He indeed squares to 6s.

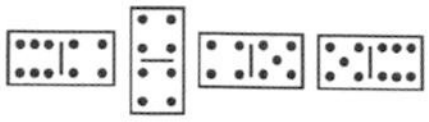

My partner rapidly plays the . West thinks about it, then plays the , so he must have at least one other 3. I must double on the 2 because I have no other tile to play. I realize that the is missing and East may have it, but I can do nothing to prevent the square. Bad luck: East does have it and plays it.

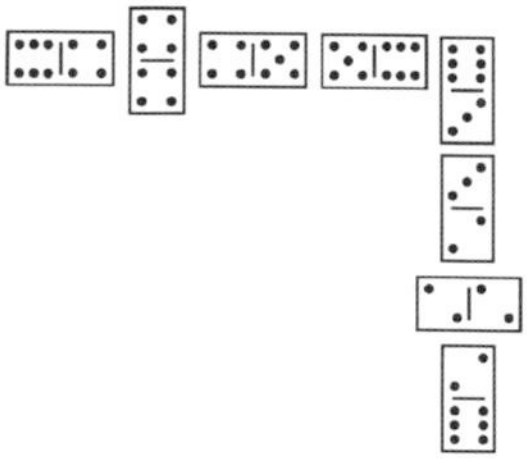

North passes this time. West now becomes the lead player and plays the rapidly. Does this mean that East has the last two 6s left?

I take some time to think over the possible plays, and to let my partner know that I have several blanks. The strongest play seems to be to repeat the 5 that I played in the first round. After I play the , East doubles with the . I take this to mean he has no 5s.

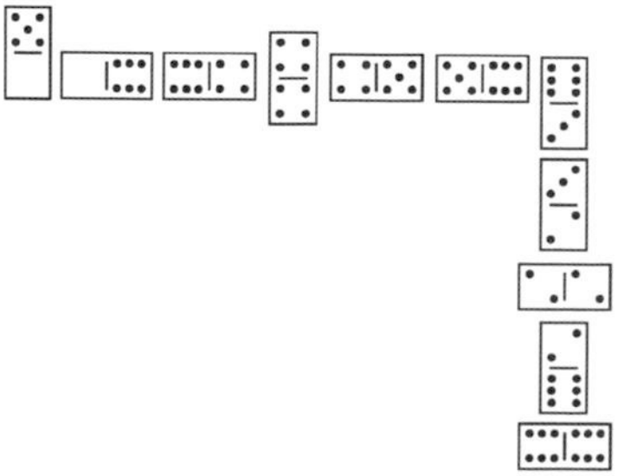

North now thinks a little and plays the . Doubling

would have been a good play, so this means the is in West's hand and (since I have the) the other 5 in my partner's hand must be the . Observe, however, that the last 6 is the and that if West has it he'll be able to jam the game. West plays the , however, so I suspect that East has the door.

I pass and the opponents now are the lead player as well as the 2nd-lead. East plays the . Repeating the opponent's suit is usually a poor play, but it's a good one in this situation since North will have to cover it.

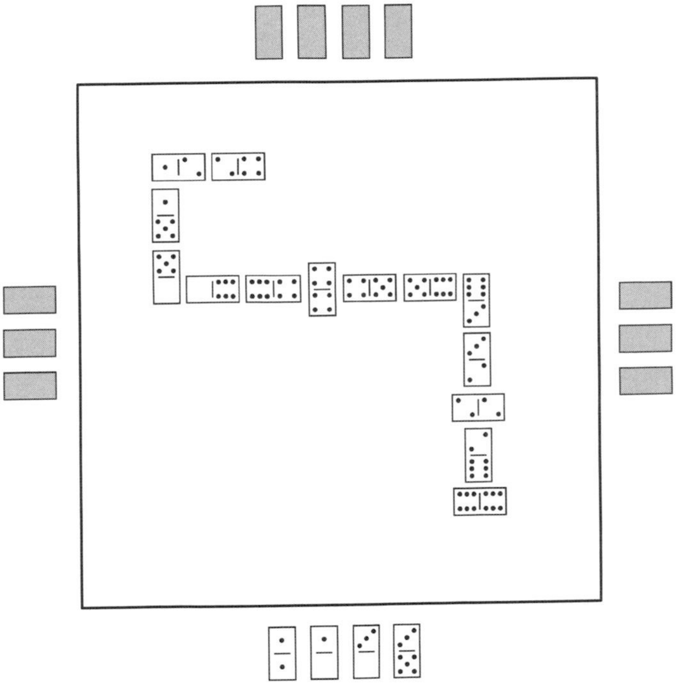

North thinks and covers his lead suit with the , repeating the 1. West rapidly plays the . I think for a while (having two 3s) then play a devastating tile: the . If I've figured the tiles out correctly, East has no 5s and will lose his door, and North will have the opportunity to hang the . But will he? After all, he doesn't know that I don't have it, and he's seen me play three 5s. If he doesn't hang it, West plays it and we're dead.

But think further: The door to the 6s is the 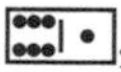, and that will be the fifth 1 played. I have the last two 1s, so North will be forced to hang the ! Sure enough, it all works out as expected.

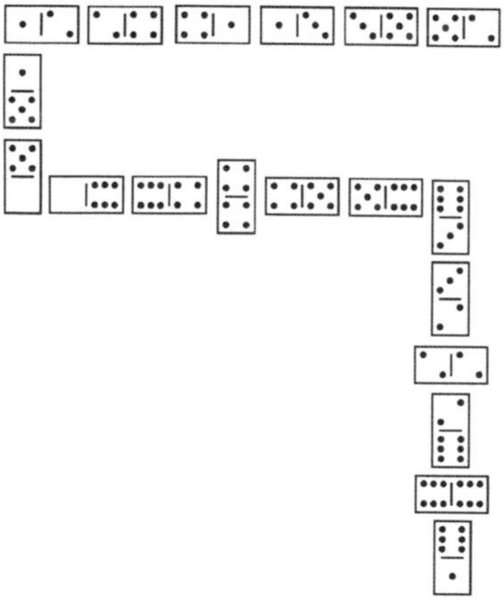

Although West remains the lead player, he's now unable to win because of his hung double. He plays the 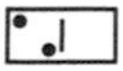 and now I have a tough decision. I can jam the game by playing the 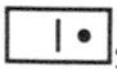, causing a general pass, then playing the . The problem is that this is not a certain win. (I'll let you work out the details, but we could possibly lose the jam 16 points to 14.) I therefore decide to play the 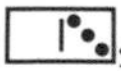, repeating my partner's second suit played. East plays the  and North the 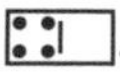.

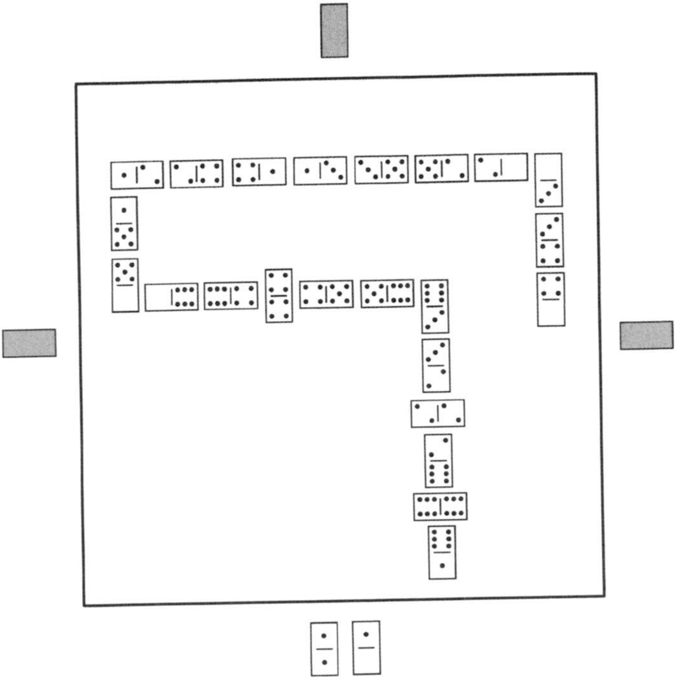

By now we know exactly who has what. North must have the 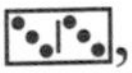, since East just hung it in the last round. West has the , and therefore East must have the 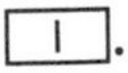. After West passes, I win by squaring to 1 with the 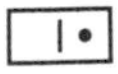 then dominating with the .

Our team wins 16 points. It turns out I would have won the jam, but I'm not too disappointed with the final result.

Game in Which I Play the Runt (East Leads)

My hand is this:

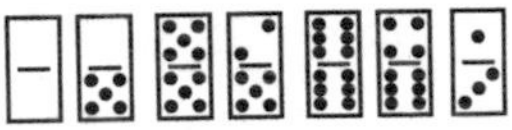

It is not a great selection. Although I'm not lacking any suit, I have three doubles and no particularly strong suit.

I am worried that the opponents may try to dominate us with the 3s, 2s, or 1s.

East leads with the 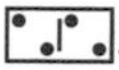. My partner (North) plays the 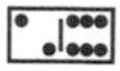 rather rapidly. Bad news: He's weak in 2s. However, I'm glad to see that he played a 6, since I have two of them including the double.

West covers the 6 with the 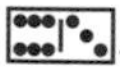. I play the  rapidly, to indicate this is my only 2.

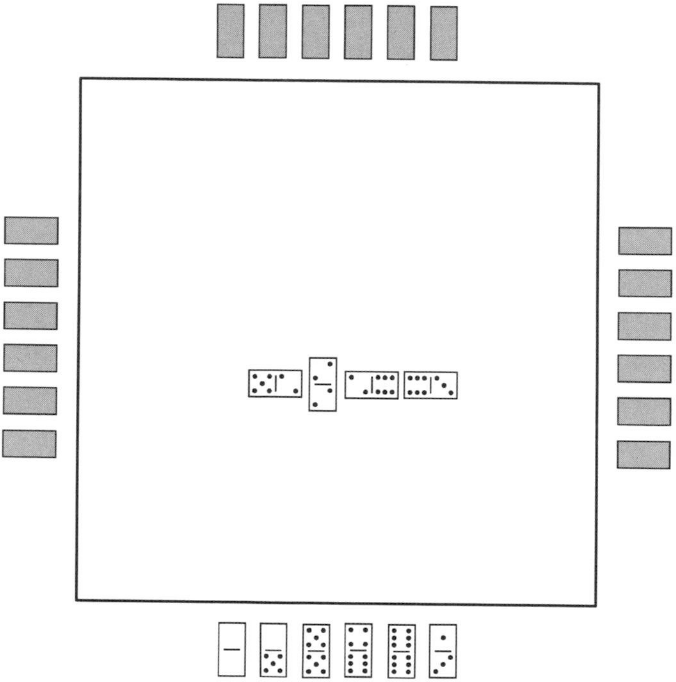

East now repeats his 2 with the 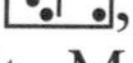, a move that confirms their dominance of this suit. My partner repeats the 6 with the . Yes! Let's see West cover that! He'll probably have to hit his partner's 2.

But contrary to my expectations he does cover the 6 with the 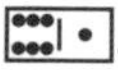. Now I'm getting very nervous as I contemplate my 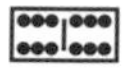 possibly getting hung. I only have one possible play, the . Although this repeats West's 3, at least it prevents the 2 from being played. This play should also tell my partner that I don't have the 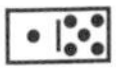 or else I'd play it now to repeat my 5.

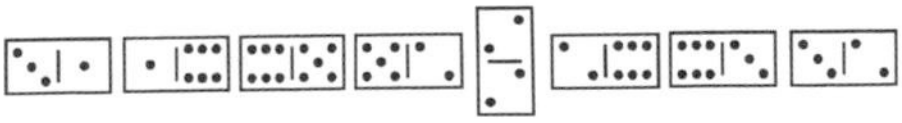

East, still the lead player, thinks for a while—then hits his 2 with the 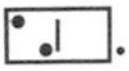. He must not have any 3s, since he had to cover his lead suit. And he probably has other blanks, since he chose to play one now.

Even better for us, the 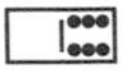 is somewhere out there, and my partner may now play it. He thinks for a long time. If he has this tile, then he's wondering if he should play it. After all, he doesn't know who has the other two 6s. He'll probably assume I have the 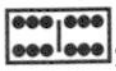, but what if East has the other one? Could the opponent be building a house with the 6?

North might also be thinking because he has the . This is a good opportunity to discard this bad tile, but he may not get any other chance to attack with the 6 if he doesn't do it now.

Maybe he feels me across the table willing him to play it, because he ends up playing the 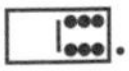.

Now West thinks a little. Perhaps he has the  and is wondering whether to double on the 3. If he does, however, he knows I might double on the 6, and his partner (having no 3s) will either pass or be forced to discard the door of the 6s (if he has it). He therefore dutifully covers the 3 and repeats his partner's blank with the 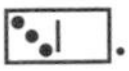.

Thanks to my partner's repeat, I have the two doors to the 6s. How can I make East pass? The  is probably a poor play, since we've already guessed he probably has at least one more blank and he won't pass to it. The 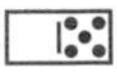 is a better play because I'm repeating my first suit, the 5.

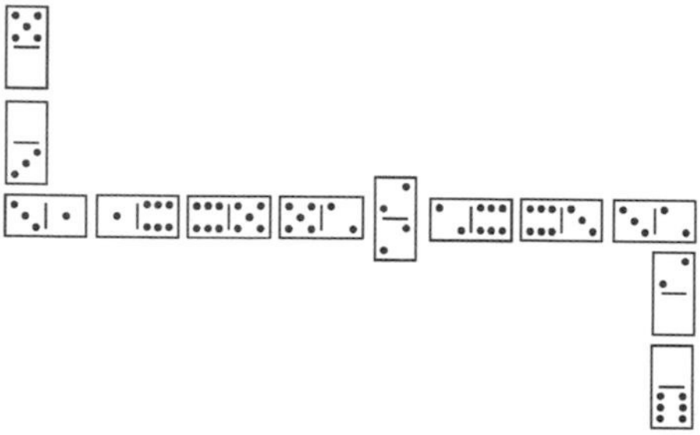

East passes. Now my partner is the new lead player, and he knows I have the last two doors to the 6s. He thinks on the 5 for quite a while, so he must have more than one 5. Let's try to figure out the possibilities. The  wouldn't allow a 2 to be played, the others would. Does he have another 3? The  comes to mind again. If he has it, it'll get hung if he plays the .

After thinking, he plays the . He either can't stop a 2 from being played (having the  and the 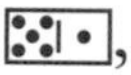, and the last 2s being the 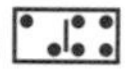 and the 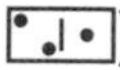), or he has the  and is afraid of his 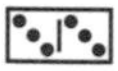 getting hung. Perhaps he's really trying to get a 4 to me so I can jam the game ("asking for the jam").

West now plays the 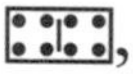, without much thought. Did he realize he was setting up a jam? Did he have any choice about it? He'd better *not* have the 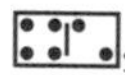, or his partner will kill him for not playing it!

Now I think about the jam. There are 110 points played after the game is jammed to 6s. The points in the hands are 168 – 110 = 58. To tie, our team must have 29 points. I have the  and the 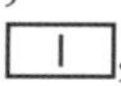, for a total of 10 points. Can my partner have 19 points in his three remaining tiles?

We already figured out he has another 5. The highest one left is the 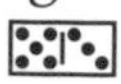 (8 points), leaving 11 points in two tiles. The two highest tiles left are the 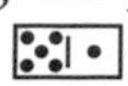 and the 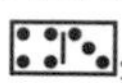, which would add up to 13 points. That means that the jam is not a sure win.

Let's also consider that on his third turn, when he played the 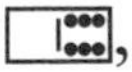, my partner thought about it. Did he have another blank? If he has just one blank we win the jam. Finally, keep in mind he did play the 4, almost as if asking for the jam. The decision is made.

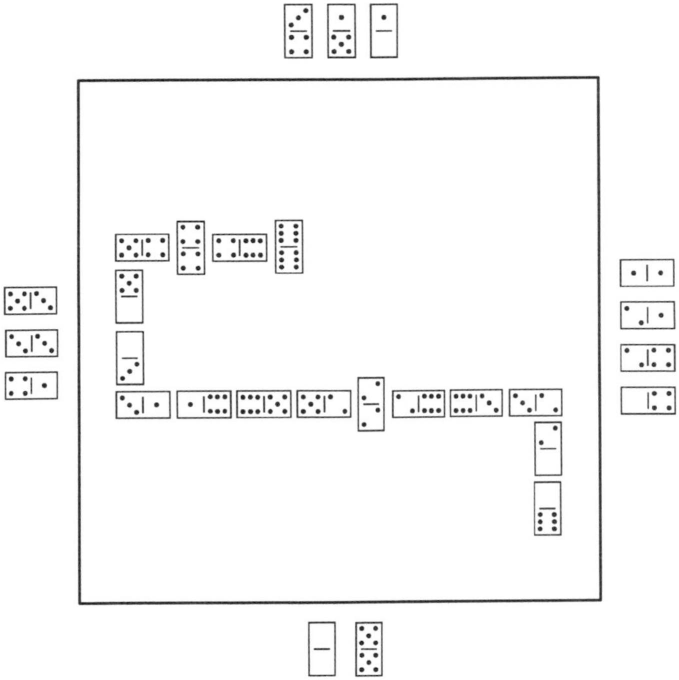

The key plays here were all done by my partner. He played and repeated three 6s in a row, giving me the last two doors. Then he signaled a jam by playing the . West made a big mistake, since he could have played the  instead of doubling with the  and letting me jam. Apparently doubling was too big of a temptation for him to resist, and he may have hoped the jamming tile was in my partner's hand.

We win the jam 24 points against their 34 points and add 58 to our total score.

APPENDIX A
Dictionary of Domino Terms

Atril—the holder for the domino tiles, usually a rectangular box.

Build a house—to play in a sneaky way, trying to confuse the opponents into developing your own suit.

Cover—to play a tile on a suit being developed by the opponents. It is primarily a defensive move.

Dominate—to win a game by discarding the last tile in one's hand.

Door—the seventh or last tile of a particular suit. If you hold this tile in your hand, no one else is able to play on that end of the skeleton. If a jam is possible, it becomes the jamming tile.

Double—a tile that has the same number suit on both ends. It is played sideways to the growing skeleton. It is generally a bad tile to have, since it may get hung.

Game—a sequence of plays that ends when a player either discards his last tile or jams the skeleton. Games earn points for the winning team.

Goat—a match in which one team loses without earning a single point. It is a source of embarrassment and mortification for the losing players.

Hand—the seven tiles selected at the beginning of a game.

Hang—to make a double unplayable by playing the other six tiles of its suit.

Jam—a play where you square with the last tile of a particular suit, making further play impossible. Each team's unplayed tiles are added, and the team with the fewest points wins all unplayed points.

Jamming tile (JT)—a tile that allows you to jam a game.

Leadoff—the first play to start a game. It is carried out by the lead player.

Lead player—the player who has the fewest tiles in his hand as the game progresses. If he doesn't pass he will win by discarding his last tile before the other players can do so.

Match—a competition made up of a series of games played by the same teams. It is generally played up to 200 points.

Pass—when a player is unable to play one of his tiles on either end of the skeleton.

Peeper—a person who sits next to the table and observes the match (see Appendix B).

Pull the hand—to play in order to develop your own suit even though your partner has fewer tiles in his hand than you do.

Repeat—to play again a suit that you are trying to develop. It is primarily an attacking move.

Round—one go-round of the table, with each player either playing one tile or passing.

Runt—the player with the most tiles in his hand, initially the 2nd-lead's partner.

2nd-lead—the player that, after the lead player, has the fewest tiles in his hand. If the lead player passes then the 2nd-lead becomes the new lead player.

Shuffle—to move the tiles so they can be mixed, prior to starting a game. This is usually the responsibility of the team that has just lost the previous game.

Skeleton—the structure made by the tiles as they're played on the table. Plays may only be made on the two open ends of the skeleton.

Square—to play a tile so that both ends of the skeleton have the same suit. It is a strong attacking move, and often the best way to make an opponent pass.

Squaring tile (ST)—a tile that allows you to square to a suit.

Table—the playing surface. Some of them are quite fancy and have built-in *atriles*.

3rd-lead—the player with the third fewest tiles in his hand, initially the lead player's partner.

Tile—a single domino piece. The set used throughout this book has 28 of them. Each one has a numerical value, equal to the sum of their two sides.

APPENDIX B
Latin Flavor

A rich tradition of Spanish slang words, phrases, and even poetry about dominoes has flourished over the years. Each country, and sometimes even regions within a country, have developed their own *sabor latino* ("Latin flavor"). I'd like to write down some of these idiosyncrasies that you may get to hear and observe around the domino table.

I. Naming the Tiles

Some of the individual tiles have their own names. Here are a few examples:

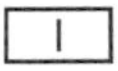 is called *La Chucha* (no translation). If you dominate with this tile, you are said to have done a *chuchazo*. Nobody minds having this light tile when a game is jammed.

 is called *Los Ojitos de Santa Lucía* ("The Eyes of Saint Lucy"), the patron saint of eye doctors.

 is known as *Cuácara con Cuácara*, a funny way to say 44.

, being the "heaviest," is the most despised double. It is called *La Vaca* ("The Cow"). Some players keep count of how many times it ends up in their hand, and use it to determine their overall luck that day.

II. Naming the Suits

Each number suit has been given many names by players. These names are usually spoken out loud when a tile is played. For example, if a 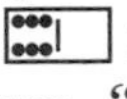 is played in order to cover a 6, the player might say: *"En blanco papel te escribo."* This translates as "on this white (blank) paper I write to you." I admit that a lot of the flavor is lost in the translation. Believe me when I say it is a rather poetic-sounding phrase. Here is how my godfather Tío Manuel might have called them:

The blanks: *En blanco papel te escribo*

The ones: *El Lunar de Lola* ("Lola's Mole")

The twos: *El Duque* ("The Duke")

The threes: *El Trisagio de Isaías* (a hymn in three parts dedicated to the Biblical prophet)

The fours: *Los Cuatro Jinetes del Apocalipsis* ("The Four Horsemen of the Apocalypse")

The fives: *Los Quintuples de Maria Elena* ("Maria Elena's Quintuplets")

The sixes: *Sixto Escobar* (a world-famous Hispanic boxer)

III. El Mirón ("The Peeper")

This is the person who sits around the table and observes the game being played. Since he can see the unplayed tiles of all players, he can always figure out the best play to make in order to win the game. He's the undisputed expert.

The well-mannered *mirón* will refrain from any comments on the plays made.

The obnoxious *mirón* will not miss an opportunity to point out the bad plays made. No one appreciates the "help" he gives.

The sneaky *mirón* will observe the strategy of the active players, hoping to get an edge on them when it's his turn to play against them.

We are all *mirones* at one time or another. You all know which category you belong to.

IV. Famous Phrases

A. *Este juego lo inventó un mudo* ("This game was invented by a mute"): This means that comments on plays should be kept to a minimum, since they might give away too much information to the player's partner.

B. *De los cobardes no se ha escrito nada* ("Nothing is ever written about the cowards"): This may be heard as a player jams the game. He is not quite sure he'll win the jam, but he's being brave and will dare this play. Good luck!

C. *Evita Perón*: Wife of Argentina's Juan Perón, and celebrated in Andrew Lloyd Webber's Broadway musical. In Spanish, "evita" means "to prevent." If a player says this phrase, he's trying to subtly tell his partner to "prevent" the opponents from playing their strong suit. Of course, he shouldn't have said it, because *Este juego lo inventó un mudo* (see above).

D. *Dale flipper* ("Use the flippers"): This phrase is accompanied by hand motions on both sides of the table, as if playing a pinball machine. It tells the opponents they need to quit their talking and shuffle the tiles.

E. *Estoy jugando con dos enemigos y un traidor* ("I'm playing against two enemies and a traitor"): An expression said by a player when he realizes his partner has double-crossed him and has been building a house or pulling the hand.

F. *Si mi abuela tuviera ruedas, fuera bicicleta* ("If my grandmother had wheels she would have been a bicycle"): This is a very useful one. When your partner starts to complain about your plays, saying "if you had played this or that we would have won," you can retort with this phrase.

V. Poetry

This last example of Latin flavor is a favorite of mine. There's a certain Alice-in-Wonderland feeling about this whimsical poem. I once heard it recited by a player who was trying to tell his partner not to jam a game, since he was loaded with points:

En lo alto de una higuera	At the top of a fig tree
Cantaba una cocolía	Precariously clinging
Y en su cántico decía	A blue crab was singing
"¡No te tires, Baldomero!"	"Don't jump, Baldomero!"

APPENDIX C
Tournament Rules

Chapter 2 introduced the rules of the game, which we have followed throughout the book. There are additional rules that apply when playing tournaments. They are designed with two purposes in mind: to penalize a player who makes a mistake and to prevent inappropriate signals between partners. For example, a player might place his leadoff tile pointing to his partner if it is a strong suit and toward the opponents if it's a bluff lead. Or a player might play a tile with his right hand to mean one thing and with his left to mean another.

To prevent such unsportsmanlike conduct, tournament rules are precise, and should be strictly adhered to. Here are the most common tournament rules as well as the usual point penalties attributed to them. When playing at home, of course, any or all of these can be ignored.

The player who shuffles the tiles must allow all others to select their tiles before picking his.

All players should place their seven tiles on their *atriles* and should not rearrange them (25 points).

Players should always play the tiles in the same fashion; that is, using the same hand and without emphasizing a play by slamming down the tile or gesturing in some other way (25 points).

The lead player must place the leadoff tile so that its long axis points to his teammate. If it is an open tile, the higher number should be away from the lead player (10 points).

If the leadoff tile is a double, the next player should place his tile on the side closer to him (10 points).

If the player faces a square (the same suit on both

sides of the skeleton), he should place the tile on either the closer end of the skeleton or on his right-hand end, whichever is appropriate (10 points).

If a tile is accidentally turned over so that another player can see it, the tile is deemed "discovered." The tile is placed face up on the table next to the player, and it must be played as soon as possible (during the player's turn). This player may dominate with this tile, but in that case, no points are awarded to the team.

If a player touches one of his tiles, he is required to play it. If he is unable to fit it on either end of the skeleton, he must place it on the table in front of him, and it becomes a discovered tile.

It is not legal to pass while holding a tile that can fit an end of the skeleton. The team is penalized and the game is played over (50 points).

If a player places a tile that does not fit on the skeleton and he quickly realizes it, he may deem it a discovered tile. If it passes unnoticed until at least one other player has taken his turn, the team is penalized and the game is played over (50 points).

Gestures, comments, or body language that may convey information (for example, tapping on the table, staring at the ceiling, a sarcastic remark) allow the opposing team to lodge a complaint. Repeated offenses may be penalized (25 points) or cause the team to be disqualified.

APPENDIX D
Further Reading

I have a highly developed sense of self-esteem, and yet I realize even I can't teach you everything about competitive dominoes. You'll find additional information in the following books. Only the first two are in English.

1. Anderson, J. and Varuzza, J.: *International Dominos*. Avid Press, Rosendale N.Y.; 1989.

This is the only English language book currently in print that talks about competitive dominoes. A few of the rules are different from those established by the International Dominoes Federation. It includes variations on the game for 2 or 3 players.

2. Müller, Reiner F.: *Dominoes: Basic Rules and Variations*. Sterling Publishing Co., Inc., New York, N.Y.; 1995.

This book teaches many games that can be played with dominoes, though competitive dominoes is not discussed. Of special interest, it includes the rules for a game called "42," which was taught to me by a Texas physician. It is very similar to bridge and even includes a version of bidding.

3. Almodovar, William: *Dominó Internacional Organizado*. Ramallo Brothers Printing Inc., Hato Rey, Puerto Rico; 1981.

This book is written by the past champion and grandmaster domino player from Puerto Rico. He explains how the International Dominoes Federation is organized, and gives the formal rules for playing in organized competitions. He teaches how to use thinking to communicate with a partner and popularized the leadoff play that carries his name.

4. Vilabella Gomez, J.M.: *ABC del Dominó*. Editorial Hispano Europea S.A., Barcelona, Spain; 1993.

Written by a Spaniard, it is unusual in its smooth style and easy readability, and for its gentle humor. The precepts it teaches are straightforward and basic. It includes a priceless story on the Chinese shoemaker who (according to legend) invented the game, which is a must-read.

5. Torres Gomez, Jose M.: *El Secreto del Dominó*. Imprenta San Rafael, Quebradillas, Puerto Rico; 1990.

This book is also full of useful information. Especially interesting is the "Mathematics of Dominoes" chapter. Like Almodovar, he's a strong believer in using the thinking conventions (which he calls the "secret" of dominoes). Unfortunately this book is out of print.

6. Gaspar Jimenez, Francisco: *Dominó a Compañeros*. Editorial Hispano Europea S.A., Barcelona, España; 1995.

I liked this book's "Ten Commandments" of playing dominoes, as well as its discussion on the luck factor. Most of the book is spent following a match of 18 games.

7. Porras, A.F.: *El Arte de las 28 Piedras*. Altolitho C.A., Caracas, Venezuela; 1997.

This is a good work that has some nice variations on plays discussed in this book. The artwork is very attractive and it has a great section on the history of dominoes.

INDEX

ABOUT THE AUTHOR

Miguel Lugo is an eye surgeon who was trained at Duke University. He has had over a dozen articles published in the fields of pathology, ophthalmology, and computers in medicine.

He was born in Aguadilla, Puerto Rico, and now lives in Maitland, Florida, with his wife, Lynette, his children, Rick, Javi, and Monica, and Sandy the Puerto Rican terrier.

Miguel Lugo won his first domino tournament at the age of 16. He's pictured below at his favorite sculpture in Philadelphia.